THE

Grace

FACTOR

BARRY COOK

THE
Grace

Why God Will *Never Give Up* on *You*

FACTOR

SAPULPA, OKLAHOMA

DEDICATION

*I*N A WORLD OF GURUS, HOMESPUN PHILOSOPHY, various religions, and self-help methods, as well as environmental stimuli, there remains a Factor—a comeback factor, a new vision initiator, an empowerment principle, a doorway of new opportunity. This factor is ages old and truly the leader's edge, the champion's belt, the winner's trophy of life. This book is dedicated to the Grace Factor himself—Jesus Christ.

CONTENTS

FOREWORD

GRACE IS A MISSING JEWEL IN THE LIVES OF MANY Christians. Too many have bought into the costly error that having begun in grace, we now work out our salvation through works. This deception has stealthily crept into the Christian mindset, causing many to believe that their acceptance with God is based on what they do, as opposed to who they are, and more importantly, who He is. Grace has become hard to believe and difficult to accept.

Sadly, it is no longer the majestic song we sing. Grace has been denuded of its raw imaginative power. As an overused word, we have gutted it of all spiritual reality. We use the word in our conversations but, for too many, it has no significant meaning. We can explain the meaning of grace. We use the fancy acronym, calling it **God's Riches At Christ's Expense**, and we can speak of it as undeserved favor, but what does that mean? And how is that grace visibly expressed in a world starving for just a little love? We can explain the word, but where is the evidence of its living reality in our midst?

Grace is the heart of the gospel—the precious missing treasure of the Church. It is the defining difference between Christianity and all other religions. Judaism, the Moslem faith, and others are all founded upon the principle of works. Man is taught that through human effort he can climb the ladder to God—that entrance into the heavenly portals is dependent on man's good works in distinction to God's love. But the stories of Jesus teach a new way. Jesus describes it as a narrow way. But it is only a narrow way because men cannot believe it is so easy. The way of human effort is a broad way because it is more believable. Christianity is the narrow way of God's marvelous love where man gets home to the Father through the tug of the Son, not the thrust of human effort. But it is wide enough to get every man through.

Unfortunately, the gospel of grace has been subtly transformed into a gospel of good works. The church defines a person's spirituality by the practice of religious activity, as opposed to the passion for a Person. He is a "good" Christian if he prays, goes to church, tithes, witnesses, and avoids certain evil activities. We have forgotten the message of Jesus—that a man's life is defined by what is in his heart, not the nature of the things he does.

We have robbed GRACE of its dignity by the repetitive reference to it without the exhilarating experience of it. Somewhere in the fields of the world, religious men buried the glorious truth of God's grace, and we must find a way to salvage this lost message. It is time to sell all that we have and go buy the field that contains this hidden booty of God's compelling love for His people.

Grace, though incredibly unbelievable, is outrageously true. Father has always loved you. He has never stopped loving you. Maybe you stopped loving yourself. Maybe you chose to believe the words of religion over the words of Jesus, but the message of grace is true. There is not a single thing you have to do in order to gain Father's love. You already have it. The loving grace of Father is reaching out from heaven, extending itself towards you with open arms and not closed fists.

How do we rediscover the riches of God's grace? How can we believe the unbelievable and accept what seems so outrageous? How can we experience that grace for ourselves?

You now hold in your hands a key to the recovery of grace for your life. Barry Cook has done the body of Christ a great favor with the release of his book, *The Grace Factor*. This is not just another teaching on grace. This is a word that emanates from the life of one who has powerfully and dramatically experienced that grace. He reminds us of what is so amazing about grace. He overcomes the resistance of those who say that it is too good to be true as he paints a picture of the sometimes offensive but always beautiful nature of God's loving grace. He takes us back to the time of beginning, and reminds us what it means to be "apprehended" by a loving God who is kind and generous and cares for us.

I invite you to open the pages of this book and allow yourself to be drawn into the world of the Grace Factor where God will receive you with open arms, fulfill your need for love, and cancel out your shame. Welcome to a brand-new world—the world of *The Grace Factor*.

—Don Milam
VP, Destiny Image Publishers
Author, *The Ancient Language of Eden*

A Word from the Author...

THIS BOOK WAS WRITTEN FOR ALL THOSE WHOSE lives have been dulled by the debilitating crush of unmet expectations; for those who feel they are too far out of reach to be helped; for those who have felt rejected by the religious crowd; for those have been marred deep in their souls by the words or actions of other people; for those who are struggling with regrets; for those who need that extra edge.

If you feel that...

- Life has given up on you;
- Life is just kicking you around;
- Your mind is overloaded;
- Distractions have derailed your faith;
- Shame and guilt continually plague your soul;
- Triumphs have lost their luster;
- Your vision has been lost to tragedy...this book is for you!

I want to warmly encourage your heart and ignite your passion for life. I want to introduce you anew to a tried-and-proven revolutionary concept. A factor—a multiplication influence—that will radically change the quality of your life.

The dedication of this book is held within the continuity of Christ alone. Solo Christos. Many make their journey without knowing what obstacles they will face in life. Challenges, tragedies, and disappointments can be daunting and sometimes paralyzing. But faith in Christ releases a grace that soothes the soul and nurtures the spirit of man.

This is the Grace Factor!

Acknowledgments

Thank you to Don Milam at Destiny Image and to Jake Jones at HonorNet for passionately embracing the message of this book and making it a reality, enabling what we do in the arena of life to echo in the halls of eternity.

Thank you to my staff—wonderful people who have proven track records of faithfulness, loyalty, and commitment to advancing the kingdom. Your great rewards lie within your own character and integrity.

Thank you to the faithful and true sons and daughters of the Ambassador Family Church body, whose support, prayers, and commitment to the vision were essential to the completion of this book.

Thank you to my family for your unconditional love and for believing that all things are possible through Christ who is our strength.

Thank you to my Executive Assistant, Rohnda Dean, who in one way or another kept me moving forward in this endeavor.

For we, having the same spirit of faith (according as it is written, "I believed, and therefore I have spoken"); we also believed and therefore speak, knowing that He who raised up the Lord Jesus shall also raise us up by Jesus, and shall present us with you. For all things are for your sake, so that the superabounding grace might be made to abound through the thanksgiving of the greater number, to the glory of God.

—2 Corinthians 4:13-15, MKJV

INTRODUCTION

But not as the offence, so also is the free gift. For if
through the offence of one many be dead, much more
the grace of God, and the gift by grace, which is by
one man, Jesus Christ, hath abounded unto many.
                                                    —Romans 5:15

*I*N WRITING TO THE ROMANS, PAUL WAS TRYING TO
lay the proper foundation of what it means to be a
Christian in a heathen culture such as the Roman Empire. The
believers in Rome had abandoned their worship of the ancient
gods of Rome that were given to mood swings, which always
demanded appeasement. They lived in fear of offending the

gods and, therefore, were very careful in their religious duties to pacify the fickle gods so as to keep them happy.

The other members of the Roman church were the Jewish converts. The Jewish believers had their roots in the Old Testament law. From children they had grown up with the commitments to keep the law even in its minutest details. They expected that the keeping of the law would cover their sins.

For each of these groups of people, Paul wanted to make sure that the image of the true God that they now served was the right image. His letter was an attempt to separate them from their false images and to present to them the one and only true God.

Paul started with the power of sin, as he wrote to both Jews and Gentiles. In the first few chapters, Paul made it clear that all have sinned and that there is no human power to break the power of sin in their lives. Appeasement of the gods and keeping the law did not deliver them from the power of sin. The sin of one man, Adam, had polluted the human race. All were born under sin and all were controlled by sin.

Once that point was clearly and dramatically made, Paul then moved to one of his favorite themes in his letters—the grace factor. In chapter five, he shot his opening salvo at the issue of sin. Paul wrote with joy and passion as he told them there was a second Adam—Christ. As the sin of Adam had dirtied the whole race, the life of Jesus had restored the whole human race. How? By the grace factor. Paul continued by saying that the grace of God, and the gift by grace, which is by one man, Jesus Christ, has abounded unto many.

While you were in sin, struggling to change your life, one man offered you a gift. If you receive this gift by simply accepting it and trusting the Giver, then your life will be powerfully and positively affected. What is the gift? It is the gift of grace flowing into your life that gives you hope for your future. This grace is not for the religious or self-righteous. It is for those who know that they desperately need a "handout" of amazing grace. It is for the prostitute standing on the corner trying to turn another trick. It is for the drug addict who is ready to pop another needle into his arm. It is for the man or woman who has just gone through the agony of divorce. It is for the young man or woman who cannot find any direction for his or her life. This grace comes wrapped in a beautiful heavenly package. Your name is lovingly written on that package with the hope that you will not return it to the Sender. This is the grace factor: God loved you so much that He sent His Son into your world— a world full of shame, guilt, and condemnation—in order that He might bring you into His world—a world of forgiveness, healing, and victory.

The grace factor is about the love of God and His Son for you. It is a story of mercy and compassion. His grace is different from the law, with all of its demands. His grace does not eliminate the law; it fulfills it by empowering you with new life and new motivation. The new life is the life of Christ, and the new motivation is the same love that He has given you. Paul wrote to the Corinthians about this love, when he said it is the love of Christ that constrains us (see 2 Corinthians 5:14). His love engulfs us and empowers us. It becomes a new source of power in our lives that frees us from sin and shame.

This is the Grace Factor!

CHAPTER ONE

THE GRACE FACTOR

What a difference between man's sin and God's forgiveness...Christ's righteousness makes men right with God, so that they can live .

—Romans 5:15, 18 TLB

*I*N ORDER TO RESOLVE THE HUMAN EQUATION, WE MUST understand the human predicament. It is not easy to be human. It is fraught with danger and trials at every level. Many enter their adult lives already carrying the baggage of huge disadvantages—psychologically impaired by abuse, educationally disadvantaged, surrounded by poverty, and ill equipped to live in this world. Having entered the world, they face rejection, endure disappointment, and struggle from one job to the next trying to find their place in life. They suffer with sickness, experience loneliness, and face many obstacles that war against the possibility of peace and success. Divorce, unemployment, financial struggles, disease, and relational conflict confront us and seek to destroy us. Within the human psyche, the soul of man struggles with guilt, shame, condemnation, insecurity, fear, anger, vengeance, bitterness, jealousy, envy, and a longing for justice.

For many people in our world, there is no hope, except for one factor—the grace factor. When you factor grace into the human equation, there is hope for the human predicament. Grace enters the darkness of our world and brings a new light of hope shining into the crevices of our dismal lives. It is only when we understand the tragedy of the human predicament that we truly can understand the value of God's grace.

Before we go any further, we must answer the question— what is grace? Too often religion causes us to warp our words through the continual repeating of truth that we have not experienced. After a while, the Word loses its power, floundering in a world of misuse.

PAUL, JESUS, AND GRACE

First, we turn to the one who probably understood grace better than anyone who has ever lived. He was a religious bigot intent on destroying the church—until that fateful day when a light from heaven knocked him off his donkey and blinded him. While lying on the ground, he was confronted by Christ. That day, grace knocked on the door of his heart, and he was introduced to the marvelous and majestic might of the love of God. You know him as the apostle Paul. In writing to the Corinthians, Paul penned these words, *For you know the grace of our Lord*

Jesus Christ, that though He was rich, yet for your sakes He became poor, that you through His poverty might become rich (2 Corinthians 8:9 NKJV).

The grace of Jesus reaches into the depth of your desperate situations in order to bring heaven's healing and the Father's favor. Grace is not a deal that you make with God. You don't have any chips to put on the table, nothing in your pockets to resolve the issues of your life. In fact, there is nothing that you can offer to God for this grace. It comes to you at no cost. When you unwrap this gift, you are looking into the eyes of Jesus. You see, grace is not a thing; it is a *person.* It is not a theological concept created in a test tube of theological studies by religious men. Grace comes to us not from the pulpit but from the person of Jesus. Jesus enters into the shadows of the human experience in order to bring us back home to

The grace of Jesus reaches into the depth of your desperate situations in order to bring heaven's healing and the Father's favor.

His Father. As Frederich Buechner wrote, "Jesus shares with us the darkness of what it is to be without God as well as showing forth the glory of what it is to be with God."[1]

Jesus brings to man a new perspective on his value and worth. Jesus gives this gift to you, offering to you a whole new look at your real value. Pointing to the birds of the air and the grass of the field and demanding your attention, He says, "*Look at the birds of the air, that they do not sow, neither do they reap, nor gather into barns, and yet your heavenly Father feeds them. Are you not worth much more than they?... But if God so arrays the grass of the field, which is alive today and tomorrow is thrown into the furnace, will He not much more do so for you, O men of little faith?*" (Matthew 6:26,30 NASB).

Jesus' grace-filled message focuses on lifting men out of the dark ditches of guilt, insecurity, and self-condemnation and causing them to see who they really are, as seen through the eyes of God. Are you not worth much more? The answer is yes.

Augustine was one of those voices speaking to us from the fourth century. Lifted from a life of moral depravity by the attractive pull of Jesus' outrageous love, he spoke compellingly on the grace and love of God. He was forever held under the sway of amazing grace, and once wrote, "My deepest awareness of myself is that I am deeply loved by Jesus Christ and have done nothing to earn it or deserve it."[2]

GRACE IS AN EMPOWERING PRESENCE AND RADICAL LOVE

Christ's grace comes to us as an empowering presence and radical love. His grace is a power, a presence, and a passion. When grace enters our lives, it brings power—a power to resolve problems, overcome tragedy, and endure hardships. His grace is also a presence—a presence that engenders confidence, creates courage, and produces peace. Finally, grace is a passion—a radical, scandalous, outrageous love—passion that secures us in the love of God, presenting a love that cannot be bought with our works but is free and outrageous.

The power of the grace of God is discovered in the presence of God. Grace as an empowering presence is emphasized in these dynamic words of God—"*I will never leave you nor forsake you*" (Hebrews 13:5 NKJV). Jesus enters into the loneliness and weakness of our lives to become our friend and to empower our lives.

The power of the grace of God is discovered in the love of God. Love is a human need. Just as we all need food and drink to survive physically, so we all need love in order to survive emotionally and psychologically. When we are deprived of love, we are deprived of life. Jesus came to renew our lives by giving us His love. *"Greater love has no one than this, that one lay down his life for his friends"* (John 15:13 NASB). Life is precious, and when one is willing to sacrifice his life, this sacrifice of love becomes the greatest expression of love. The life that He gave us was a love—a love that gave us life.

TREASURES IN EARTHEN VESSELS

But we have this treasure in earthen vessels, that the surpassing greatness of the power may be of God and not from ourselves; we are afflicted in every way, but not crushed; perplexed, but not despairing; persecuted, but not forsaken; struck down, but not destroyed (2 Corinthians 4:7-9 NASB). This is the power of grace manifesting itself in the trials and tribulations of life. It does not protect us from the troubles of life, as some Christians have been led to believe, but it keeps us in the midst of our difficulties. In verse one, Paul said that as we have received mercy, we do not lose heart. Mercy is grace manifested to us in another form. Mercy is the great treasure that God gives to mankind. Mercy is getting a verdict on our lives that we do not necessarily deserve. Mercy is benevolence, kindness, and favor so strong that they are morphed into our lives as a power that causes us to stand strong in the midst of life's tragedies.

Mercy is getting a verdict on our lives that we do not necessarily deserve.

Everything in God's kingdom is focused on God's grace. Throughout the earlier chapters of Paul's letter to the Romans, he emphasizes the tragic pull of sin. Man is under the controlling and compelling undertow of sin that is pulling him further and further away from the shores of God's loving arms. Sin destroys lives and at the same time separates man from the only hope to save his life. This separation is created by man's flight from the presence of God. Seeking healing in all the wrong places, man continues to drift further and further away.

THE GRACE FACTOR REVEALED IN THE HUMAN DRAMA

It is a tragic story, but into the human drama, God has introduced His Son who dives into the dark waters of human misery and in a heroic, selfless effort brings man back to the shore of God's love. In his letter to the Romans, Paul introduces the irresistible magnetism of grace. The majesty of God's grace is that He demonstrated His love toward us, even while we were sinners. Romans 5:8 says, *But God demonstrates his own love for us in this: While we were still sinners, Christ died for us* (NIV). While we were still messed up, in the middle of life's stuff, when we did not have all of our ducks in a row, it was at that time that He manifested His love for us by paying the ultimate sacrifice. We are all used to getting what we deserve. That is the nature of the world in which we live. Rewards come with effort and work. But God's love is presented to us as a free gift. Well, it is free in the sense that it doesn't cost us anything, but it did cost heaven a lot! In fact, even when we were snotty little kids, undeserving of a lick of kindness, Christ came to us offering His hand of mercy, extending it to us while He was nailed to a wooden cross.

Not only does He rescue us out of the torment of transgressions, but also—as we see in 1 Corinthians 1:2—He now proclaims that we are "saints" of the Most High God. Now, maybe you don't see the dramatic significance of those words. We are used to cruising over the important things of the Scriptures as we search for the "deeper" revelations. Well, here is one of those deeper revelations that most will miss. As Paul sits down to pen this letter, he addresses the saints at Corinth as "saints." Yet in later paragraphs, he is going to expose their spiritual nakedness. He is going to reveal their sectarian spirit, their misuse of the gifts, their carnality, and their failure to be everything God has called them to be—yet he calls them saints. **This is the grace factor.** Grace factors into the human equation and calls things that "are not" as though "they are." The eyes of grace see you and judge you in a different way and by a different criterion than man. Man looks on the outward appearance, but God looks on the heart.

Grace factors into the human equation and calls things that "are not" as though "they are."

CHRISTIANITY IS NOT ABOUT OUR DO'S AND DON'TS—IT'S ABOUT THE SPIRIT OF GOD

Our focus must be on Jesus Christ. Christianity is about relationship, not just following rules. If you simply come to Christ and then continue to try to resolve the issues of your life by attempting to be good, you will fail. The great secret to Christianity is in the exchanged life. In Galatians 2:20, Paul said *it is no longer I* who control my life (NKJV). He found another power, and that was Christ living through him. It's not dependent on what we can or can't do, but it is dependent on what He can do through us. This is the grace factor.

If you focus on what you can't do, you'll never get to where you're supposed to be going. You'll never get there by your own works. And if it's your own works that got you there, then your own works aren't worth anything before God anyhow. Does this sound confusing? If it isn't based on what I am supposed to do or what I can't do, then how should I live my life? What am I supposed to do?

You're supposed to let His grace have its perfect work on the inside of you. You are supposed to accept what He has already done for you. You are supposed to learn how to rest in His works. In the book of Genesis, we see that God worked six days, and everything that He did was called "good." Man's first full day was the seventh day, the day of rest. Man began his life in the rest of what God had done. It is not what you have done, but it is what He has done that makes you "good."

THE TWO LAWS IN THE UNIVERSE—THE LAW OF ADAM AND THE LAW OF CHRIST

What is the proper response to the grace of God? If God is going to love me in spite of myself, then why should I give up? Why wouldn't I want to praise Him? He's going to love and accept me anyway. He's going to have mercy on me anyway. When everybody else rejects me, He's not going to reject me. He's going to love me anyway. The ways of God are paradoxical. God says that you're free from the law. But you say, "Yeah, but my old sin nature sure seems to be alive and working well. I can't seem to overcome sin." What does God do in response? He rises up on the inside of you and says, "I'll take care of that too. I'll nail it on the cross with Me. All your badness (and all your goodness) is nailed to the cross and declared to be dead." When you arrive in God's kingdom, you are DOA, dead on arrival. You have died with Christ, and now you have a new life based on the power of Christ living in you.

There are two laws in the spiritual universe—the law of Adam and the law of Christ. Through Adam, sin entered into the world and brought death. Through Christ, grace entered into the world and brought life. This message of grace was the great controversy between Paul and the Jews. The Jews thought that their works were justified, but Paul declared that they were not and never could be. Don't be too hard on the Pharisees, because many of you sometimes live as though your works justify you, but they don't. You're justified by faith in His grace. You are qualified to be partakers of His divine nature because of the grace of God. The law of Christ, which is the law of grace, has broken the power

You're justified by faith in His grace.

of the law of Adam, which is the law of sin. Paul made this truth very clear in his letter to the Romans.

> *Therefore, just as through one man sin entered into the world, and death through sin, and so death spread to all men, because all sinned—for until the Law sin was in the world; but sin is not imputed when there is no law. Nevertheless death reigned from Adam until Moses, even over those who had not sinned in the likeness of the offense of Adam, who is a type of Him who was to come. But the free gift is not like the transgression. For if by the transgression of the one the many died, much more did the grace of God and the gift by the grace of the one Man, Jesus Christ, abound to the many. And the gift is not like that which came through the one who sinned; for on the one hand the judgment arose from one transgression resulting in condemnation, but on the other hand the free gift arose from many transgressions resulting in justification. For if by the transgression of the one, death reigned through the one, much more those who receive the abundance of grace and of the gift of righteousness will reign in life through the One, Jesus Christ. So*

*then as through one transgression there resulted
condemnation to all men, even so through one act
of righteousness there resulted justification of life to
all men.*

—Romans 5:12-18 NASB

God's grace has covered your sin through His work on the cross. His blood has justified you, made you acceptable before God. His blood has reconciled you to God by breaking through the wall of sin. You don't have any reason not to call upon the Lord Jesus Christ as your Savior, because He has already made provision for you in every area of your life.

YOU ARE A MASTERPIECE

Not only are you a saint, but you are also a divine masterpiece. In Ephesians 2:10, He said, "You're my workmanship." What does that mean? That means God will work it out. God will take the sketch of sin and sadness that has been your life and turn it into a portrait of purity and power.

The reason that you might not experience this spiritual reality is that no one ever told you. You are still living under the same illusion that it all depends on you. You don't have a revelation of the grace factor. You haven't come to the realization that you are never going to be good enough to get there. You're never going to do enough things right to get there. You haven't come to the realization that God's got you in His hand and He will never let go.

You must come to the realization that your life is no longer the same. It is a masterpiece of His grace. When you come to that realization, then you will begin to trust that He is going to see you all the way to the other side. Though your mind may be weary today, you know that you're going to the other side of something. You're Christ's workmanship. You're created for good works. You may say, "Well, I don't feel like my works are always good." They're not. Don't fall back into the old trap of the Pharisees. It is not about you. It is about Him! It is about what He has done *for* you and will do *through* you. This is the grace factor. Second Corinthians 5:21, says that you've been made righteous, and He calls you holy. "Well, I don't feel so holy and righteous," you say. That's the problem. It is not about how you feel; it is about who He is in you. It is not about who you think you are; it is about who He says you are. Does God lie? If He says you are holy and have been made righteous, then simply accept God's verdict on your life.

IT'S GOING TO BE ALL RIGHT

Who made you the way you are? God. Jesus Christ paid a price to make you a saint. "But how many miracles have I done?" you may ask. Well, you don't do miracles—God does them *through* you. And He will do them for anybody who believes. Matter of fact, He'll do it for some people when they're not even believing. Why? It is because God is rich in mercy—abundantly rich in mercy. Ephesians 1:6 says that you're fully accepted. God isn't holding anything back from you. Every promise that He gave in the Book is yours. He's not waiting until you reach a certain level of spirituality to pour out His power on you and give you success. He says no to that kind of thinking. You're fully accepted **now.**

"That can't be true," you say. By the blood of Jesus Christ it's true. "It doesn't make sense to me. I mean, I know what I am." But He does too. That's why He sent Jesus. If it were up to you, you would have never gotten out of your mess.

"What am I supposed to do then?" you ask. You're supposed to accept what He has done for you and then thank Him. So if you don't have anything else to thank God for, you can thank Him because you called on the name of the Lord Jesus Christ and put your trust in His blood—not your own abilities, not your own sound mind, not your past, not your upbringing, and not what you've gone through. You have put your trust in God, and He's already promised that you're going to be all right. It might not always look like it is going to be all right, but in the end, when the final chapter of your life is written, it will be all right.

Your outward man might be perishing a little bit, and you might be going through difficult and depressing times, but everything will be all right. Jesus will be your peace in the midst of that storm.

Unfortunately, sometimes when we get into the middle of a storm, we forget that God loves us and is there with us. The storm clouds of life's situations might obscure His presence, but do not be deceived by your circumstances. God is there, and at any moment the light of His presence will break through the dark clouds that seem to hide His face. This is the grace factor. His presence is always there, even when we feel like we cannot see Him. The problem comes when we get nervous and think that He won't come. So then we take over our storm protection services and try to work things out for ourselves. Well, that is the beginning of more problems. Just ask Abraham about trying to fulfill God's promises through your own efforts. Be careful, or you just might give birth to an Ishmael and create a whole new set of problems.

The storm clouds of life's situations might obscure His presence, but do not be deceived by your circumstances. God is there.

When you put your life in the hands of God, you may not always understand everything that you're going through. The devil might get his hand in the middle of it. You might make some dumb decisions. But wherever you are and whatever you're going through, God knows it and He is working all things together for your good. What the devil meant to destroy you, God will use to deliver you.

Now, I can just hear somebody saying, "Well, I just think you're hyping up some things." The truth of the matter is that you can never out-hype God. Things are always bigger and better than any words we can use to describe God's presence and power that is at work in our lives.

GIFTS ARE FREE!

First Corinthians 12 tells us that the gifts of the Spirit are for everybody. That's why Paul called them gifts. You understand that almost everything that God has given us comes at no cost to us. God lavishly pours out His love and mercy on us at no cost. *He isn't trying to charge you for anything!* You couldn't have paid for it anyway. You can kill as many lambs, goats, and calves as you want, and it will not make you free or deliver you from the guilt of your sin. I can hear somebody saying, "I just don't have faith. This is just too good to be true. Surely there is something that I must do." The truth of the matter is that you don't have enough faith. Even the faith that you have is a gift. You are at a crossroads, and either you will believe that the gifts are free and simply accept them in the love in which they were given, or you will continue to live your life trying to be perfect and spiritual. But don't take these things lightly. *Or do you think lightly of the riches of His kindness and forbearance and patience, not knowing that the kindness of God leads you to repentance?* (Romans 2:4 NASB). The problem for most Christians is that they have placed a low value on the kindness and goodness of God. They have believed the misrepresentation of God that is preached in too many pulpits. They have never experienced the overwhelming, passionate love of God who wishes to extravagantly bless them and enrich their lives.

How many of you have tried and tried to resolve things in certain areas of your life and nothing gets better? The problem is that you don't believe the party is for you and that all those gifts God has put on the table are yours. If you put your faith and trust in God's grace and begin to unwrap those gifts, you will discover that you have been given power that can release you from your bondages. You have been given strength that will help you when you are in the midst of troubling times, and wisdom that will give you direction when you are confronting baffling situations. It doesn't matter if you're in the middle of one of those scenes right now. You can be sitting in the middle of your situation and say, "God, I need Your help to get out of here." He will get you out of there, or He will get you through it.

Some of you may be saying, "I just feel bad about telling God I'm sorry and then going back and doing this kind of stuff again." You know what? He feels bad about it too. He knew that a lot of us were going to be knuckleheads and continue to do the same old things over and over again. So He said, "You know what? I'm not going to try to negotiate with them, because I'll always lose. So I'm just going to *cover* it all for them, and *credit* it to them as righteousness."

HIS GOODNESS LEADS YOU TO REPENTANCE

The Bible says Elijah was tempted with passions just like ours. It doesn't say on all points he was like Jesus. Jesus was tempted, but in all points He was found to be without sin. The Bible doesn't say that about Elijah. It says Elijah was tempted just like we are tempted, yet he prayed and God answered.

I can hear you asking, "What about repentance?" See, the goodness of God will lead you to repentance. It is His goodness, His concern for you, that provides a way for you to turn around and go back to the Father's house. He was with you the whole journey—He never left you. He loves you, and you can trust Him. The goodness of God will lead you to repentance. That's why He said you're His workmanship, created for good works. God is working it out in you.

Second Peter 1:1 says that *we have obtained like precious faith*. Peter was saying, that we have the same faith that he had. It's resident within us. But you say, "Well, I can't grow my faith." Of course you can grow your faith. You can read and hear the Word of God, and it will give you knowledge of Him and cause you to grow and increase. Second Peter 1:3 says that He *has given to us all things that pertain to life and godliness* (NKJV). Jesus said it's already yours. Sometimes we just don't seem to know it. So what keeps us from getting it?

BLOCKED BY YOUR SIN AND GUILT

What primarily holds you back is your consciousness of sin and the guilt that hangs out in your soul, telling you that you're not worthy enough to receive what God has given. You don't think you're worthy enough for God to give it to you. You think you've got to attain a certain place and then God will anoint you. No. He sent that anointing to help you get free. He didn't send it as a reward for your self-righteousness. He sent it to make you holy. He sent it to help you get through and to break the heavy bonds. He sent it to knock off the wickedness that comes in your life, to break you free from darkness, to speak to you, and to lead and guide you into all truth. When Jesus was talking with His disciples right before He was to go to the cross, He told them that He was going to give them a gift. God sure does love giving gifts. He told them that He was going to give them the Holy Spirit, and that the Holy Spirit would be with them and guide them. Jesus told them that it would be like having Him there with them all the time. What a wonderful God!

MERCY AND TRUTH HAVE MET EACH OTHER

In Psalm 85:10, David says, *Mercy and truth have met together; righteousness and peace have kissed each other* (NKJV). Mercy and truth usually don't mix too well. They are the ultimate oxymoron, the extreme opposites. But in God, opposites attract. His truth was attracted to His mercy, and mercy won the debate. When Jesus died on the cross, mercy and truth had a meeting. Truth said you deserve what you get. You should be punished for your actions. Mercy said there is another way, and it is the way of compassion. Mercy said, "I will give them my grace, and by my grace they will be brought back into the arms of my Father.

The demands of God's truth about your actions were met through the blood of Jesus Christ. He resolved your transactions so that God could justify you *freely* before Him.

Legalism demands that we fulfill the burdens of our sin through some means of penance, but as we have all learned, there is nothing we can do to remove the guilt or the consequences of our sin. We need help from another dimension; from another power that can cancel our debt and remove our guilt. From the eternal warmth of the "communion of glory" with His Father, the Son of Man descended into the cold abyss of human misery. This holy strategy necessarily included His being stripped of any divine advantage. He exited through the bright light of heaven's gate—an exit witnessed by the consternation of hosts of angels—and entered into the misery and hopelessness that circumscribed the existence of humankind.

Into our world, He came to enact the plan of the Father that would resolve our powerlessness in the face of sin's grip on us. That plan was the grace factor. What we could not do, Jesus did. The only thing left for us to do is to *trust* and *accept* what He has done.

TRUST AND THE GRACE FACTOR

In Proverbs 3:5,6, Solomon offers these words of encouragement. *Trust in the Lord with all your heart, and lean not on your own understanding; in all your ways acknowledge Him, and He shall direct your paths* (NKJV).

These wise words should be incentive enough to put your trust in God and acknowledge that He is well able to direct your path in life. The word *direct* comes from a word that means "to smooth out, to break through a barrier, to clear out before you." He

> *God's grace helps us in times of need, and sees us through the pressures of life.*

is the God of breakthrough, clearing a path that will open up a way into God's divine destiny for your life.

Another way of saying it is that God goes before you and clears the garbage out of your path. You say, "I don't feel like He's cleared much out of my life." Well, He never said you wouldn't go through some stuff. But consider what Paul says in Hebrews 4:16. *Let us therefore draw near with confidence to the throne of grace, that we may receive mercy and may find grace to help in time of need* (NASB). God's grace helps us in times of need, and sees us through the pressures of life.

The Lord prepared a table for us in the presence of our enemies (see Psalm 23:4), so that means the only way to get to that table is to face some enemies. Sometimes when we choose to run from our enemies, we lose the opportunity of eating

from the table that God prepares for us in the valley of our pain. If we avoid being in the presence of our enemies, we miss out on what God has prepared for us. Some of you are avoiding your enemies, and some of you are turning away from uncomfortable circumstances and situations. Some of you are pulling back from everyone and everything in an effort to avoid being hurt. But God says, "Go on and walk in there. I have a meal for you in the middle of the desert of your despair."

Grace teaches you to trust your Lord, knowing that He will never leave you alone. He has prepared a table for you in the presence of your enemies. He will force His favor right in the face of your enemies. God prepares a sumptuous table, with blessings, provision, and all the things you need. Whatever your enemy is or whatever is coming against you, there is a table ready for you. But you can only get to that table by putting your faith in God. You must believe that He is a good God and that He has only good things planned for you. You must choose to trust Him to get you out of your problems, instead of depending on your own strategies. Trust opens the door to the grace factor.

JOSEPH AND THE GRACE FACTOR

You will remember that because of a dream, a God-given dream, Joseph reaped the wrath of his brothers and was sold into slavery. While in Egypt, he was falsely accused by the wife of his boss and thrown into prison. While living in that prison, all he had was a dream, but that dream became a nightmare. Where was the God of his dreams? Why had God let him down? Why had He forsaken him? Eventually, Joseph found the table in the presence of his enemies, and became the second leading ruler in Egypt. God had not forsaken him. Joseph's brothers had betrayed him. He had been lied to, forsaken, imprisoned, and lost, but he was not lost to God. God led him through the trail of troubles, and brought him to the throne.

Grace brought him to glory. Now, that is a lesson you must never forget. The grace of God will take you places that you will never be able to reach on your own. You must trust God in the midst of your circumstances, because He is weaving a cloak of favor for you that will bring glory into the darkness of your life. This is the grace factor.

The grace of God will take you places that you will never be able to reach on your own.

GRACE LEADS TO GLORY

When you have the blessings of God on your life, you have found the grace factor. When you put your hand in the hand of God, you will find the grace factor. When you accept His grace, you will discover His power and glory. This all happens when you say, "God, I'm going to walk with You through thick and thin. I'm going through because I trust in You. You have good things planned for me, and want only the best for my life. Even when I don't understand what's going on, Your favor still follows me and has a table for me."

When you're in the middle of trials, being persecuted and feeling perplexed, God wants you to know that you can have His grace. Remember Paul's words, *We are afflicted in every way, but not crushed; perplexed, but not despairing; persecuted, but not forsaken; struck down, but not destroyed* (2 Corinthians 4:8,9 NASB). The word *perplexed* means "embarrassed, puzzled, bewildered, complicated, and confused." The word *persecuted* means "to harass, afflict, or burn down." The phrase, *struck down* means "to be hit with force, to smite, to stab, to pierce, and to move in a direction by hitting." Paul is saying that when he got in the middle of some serious stuff, he learned how to apply the grace factor. He kept his eyes on what others could not see. He knew that grace would lead to a glory beyond anything anyone could imagine.

I know there is a grace factor in my life that guarantees I'm going to make it to the other side. I may not know everything I need to know, and I may not always say everything I need to say. I may make some mistakes along the way and get into some serious trouble. But I have learned that darkness is only a shadow created by passing clouds, and when those clouds have passed by, then the marvelous light of God's glory will return.

I DON'T DESERVE IT

In light of all of this, you might be tempted to think that you just don't deserve all of this favor. Well, the truth of the matter is that you don't deserve it. The grace factor has nothing to do with whether you deserve it or not. It has to do with who God is, not who you are. The grace factor is released in your life by what Jesus did for you.

Natural strength does not work with the grace factor. Flesh begets flesh and spirit begets spirit. God says this isn't about you. There's nothing you can do to attract the grace factor.

Robert Farrar Capon described this aspect of the grace factor in this way. "And if there is a God who can take the dead and, without a single condition of credit-worthiness or a single, pointless promise of reform, raise them up whole and forgiven, free for nothing—well, that would not only be wild and wonderful; it would be the single piece of Good News in a world drowning in an ocean of blame."[3] In a world struggling to get approval and find a way to change their lives, this is truly good news. It does not depend on you! You are not the savior of your own soul! There is one who has come to bring power and purpose for your life, and these come to you through the vehicle of grace. The grace factor is based on the nature of God and His love for you. He is the initiator and you are the recipient. You are not seeking Him. He is seeking you.

The grace factor is *for* you when the facts are *against* you. Grace is there when you run out of time. In fact, that is when grace is at its best. At the last moment, in the nick of time, grace comes to rescue you from your messes, even if those messes are self-created.

The grace factor is for you when the facts are against you.

God will change whatever He needs to change to get you wherever He needs to take you. You may not even understand where you are right now. You might think you are messed up. You might think you are in the middle of something you can't get out of, but you must understand that God knows where you are, and He is bringing you to the other side. The things that you think are doing you harm and making you worse, God is working for your good. He is the grace factor.

God will get you to your destiny if you will trust in Him. God will see you all the way through it if you will trust in Him. When it looked like you were pulling away and seemed as if God would not have anything else to do with you, He was right there. He is that fourth man in the fire. Quit looking at the flames—look around and you will find Him. He is right there in the middle. He is the grace factor. For you see, grace is not an object, but it is a person. The grace factor is Jesus. When you are looking for the grace factor, you will find it at the feet of Jesus.

He is apprehending you with His love and mercy, and He is saying, "Hey, will you put your hand back in My hand today? I am not mad at you, and I'm not holding anything against you. I fully accept you, so just put your hand in Mine, for I am the grace factor."

Jesus is the grace factor, and His actions are in perfect harmony with His words. No contradiction existed to create confusion or disappointment in those who followed Him. His life was a living symbol of the very words He spoke. He was a book read of all men. The love of the Father was fleshed out in His daily associations with the very lowest in the caste system of society and religion. He ate meals with the untouchables, defended the prostitutes, healed the afflicted, and pursued the oppressed. He didn't do this to try to make a statement. He preferred these people. He truly enjoyed their company. And, in turn, they were all at ease in Jesus' presence; all, that is, except the religious leaders who despised this reversal of established order in their precious community.

Jesus is the grace factor, and His actions are in perfect harmony with His words.

Grace comes to us in the person of Jesus, and it comes to those who know that they need it, not to those who are seeking to perfect themselves through religious ways. The grace of Jesus is for the broken, the hurting, the rejected, and the disillusioned ones. His grace is for everyone. His grace is for you.

Grace IN ACTION

God demonstrates His own love toward us, in that
while we were still sinners, Christ died for us. Much
more then, having now been justified by His blood,
we shall be saved from wrath through Him.
—Romans 5:8,9 NKJV

When you truly understand the implications of this passage, you will understand that you have been made righteous through the blood of Jesus Christ. This is the grace factor, and it has nothing to do with what you have done but everything to do with what Jesus Christ has done for you. His blood purified you and made you acceptable before God, qualifying you to be a partaker of His divine nature.

As recipient of His love and grace, you must spend time with Him every day, praising Him and allowing His power, presence, and passion to fill your life and meet your needs. Then you must live your life in such a way that everyone you meet will recognize that you have something they need and want.

CHAPTER TWO

WHAT IS SO AMAZING
ABOUT GRACE?

And when He had taken some bread and given
thanks, He broke it, and gave it to them, saying,
"This is My body which is given for you; do this in
remembrance of Me."

—Luke 22:19 NASB

HE TABLE OF THE LORD IS TO BE A TABLE WHERE
memories are resurrected and thanksgiving is
offered. Loss of memory is a common problem,
and we all have a tendency to forget the good things that have
happened in our lives and the good things that others have done

for us. Life has a way of just speeding by us, and we easily become distracted by the daily routines of life that obscure the memories of those precious moments that have intersected our lives. We just don't take time to savor the moments that really count. Our lives are on cruise control. Most of us have chosen to live on the surface realities of life, never diving deeper in an effort to discover what is happening in the deeper core of our being.

At that celebrated table, as the disciples were gathered around Jesus, He introduced the loaf and the cup in preparing to participate in the historic Passover celebration. As His hands touched the bread and then reached for the cup, the Passover celebration was forever changed. The disciples had eaten the Passover meal many times, but this one was different. Jesus established that moment in eternity, and told His disciples to appreciate the celebration every time they celebrated it in the future. Every time we gather at this table, we should do it in memory of Him. We should be able to resurrect memories of experiences with Christ—memories of those moments that changed our lives.

Stop in the midst of your daily routine and seize the moment. That was His message. Allow yourself to penetrate through the cloud of consciousness floating around the upper levels of your thinking. Then guide your reflections towards the deeper places in your soul and allow yourself to discover new levels of spiritual contemplation, considering all that He has done for you. Do this in memory of Him!

In the next few hours following that Passover celebration, Jesus would endure the most horrific agony that any man would ever endure. Those whom He came to save would reject Him and then murder Him in the most hideous way imaginable. Hanging on the tree suspended between heaven and earth, His life would be given for all mankind. As Robert Farrar

Capon wrote, "The Word who makes the world is identical to the Word who saves the world... He brings his Divinity down into the misery of our humanity, and he lifts that very misery up into himself. He who is the key to the city dies outside the city."[1]

He paid the necessary price so that we could experience the ultimate life.

He paid the *necessary price* so that we could experience the *ultimate life.* This is truly amazing grace.

AMAZING GRACE, HOW SWEET THE SOUND

And you were dead in your trespasses and sins, in which you formerly walked according to the course of this world, according to the prince of the power of the air, of the spirit that is now working in the sons of disobedience. Among them we too all formerly lived in the lusts of our flesh, indulging the desires of the flesh and of the mind, and were by nature children of wrath, even as the rest. But God, being rich in mercy, because of His great love with which He loved us, even when we were dead in our transgressions, made us alive together with Christ (by grace you have been saved), and raised us up with Him, and seated us with Him in the heavenly places, in Christ Jesus, in order that in the ages to come He might show the surpassing riches of His grace in kindness toward us in Christ Jesus. For by grace you have been saved through faith; and that not of yourselves, it is the gift of God; not as a result of works, that no one should boast."

—Ephesians 2:1-9, NASB

People who are still bound by the shackles of sin and the stress of their shame have never encountered the amazing grace that flows from the cross of Jesus. They might have had personal encounters with religion—religion that propagates the bad news of guilt and condemnation—but they have never experienced the mighty ocean of God's amazing grace. People who feel like they can make it to heaven through their own works don't really understand the need for grace, and they have never really put their faith in Jesus Christ. Because they don't understand that no one can ever be good enough to make it on their own, they only have faith in what they can do on their own. They have never met the God who is abundantly rich in mercy and grace. They might be able to describe grace, talk about grace, and quote verses about grace, but they have never experienced it. They have no concept of what grace is all about. How sad!

When I start preaching about grace and mercy, there are always people who say it seems too easy, too good to be true. The world has a saying: If it *looks* too good to be true, it *is* too good to be true! I'm sure you've discovered, as I have, that most of the time, this is a *true* statement. But when it comes to the grace of God, this axiom loses its punch. Though it sounds too good to be true, God's grace is for real. His grace cannot be bought with all your religious works. There is nothing you can do to make Him love you any more than He already does. Now, that is what I call good news!

There is nothing you can do to make Him love you any more than He already does.

This is truly amazing. I get what I don't deserve. The indictment against me has been cancelled out through His death, burial, and resurrection. The barrier reef separating me from God has been wiped out by a tsunami of amazing grace.

JUST A LITTLE BIT OF TRUST—
THAT'S ALL THAT HE ASKS

Now not for his sake only was it written, that it was reckoned to him, but for our sake also, to whom it will be reckoned, as those who believe in Him who raised Jesus our Lord from the dead (Romans 4:23,24 NASB). Paul was talking about Abraham. In the face of an impossible promise—that in the late years of his life, he would have an heir—Abraham stood strong in the face of conflicting circumstances. God converted, exchanged, and transformed Abraham's trust into righteousness. The exchange rate for human trust is imputed righteousness. You can cash it in at any time. You turn in your trust to the divine cashier and righteousness is paid back to you. This is a great deal offered by Christ to all men.

Paul goes on to say that the promise of righteousness was not only for Abraham but could be experienced by all who would trust in God. Romans 5:1 says, *Therefore having been justified by faith, we have peace with God through our Lord Jesus Christ* (NASB). You say, "What can I do to find serenity for my tormented conscience and peace for my troubled circumstances?" There are no self-help books that can lead you to the place you are seeking, no good deed that you can do, and no deal you can make with God. There is no lottery that you can win to alleviate your pain. There is only one key to open the door to the pastures of peace. The key is simply to trust Him. Put your trust in who He is and what He has already done, and it will be yours. Now, that's what's so amazing about grace.

You don't have peace because you're so holy and good; you have peace because of what Jesus did for you. You don't have harmony in your life because you have blocked from your mind all the things that have created discord in your soul. You can't keep pushing down the rejection, disappointment, and pain that have come into your life and think that this is the way to peace. It might create a semblance of peace at the upper levels of your consciousness, but in the lower levels of your soul, the turmoil is raging and ready to erupt at any moment.

The solution is to simply turn from your own feeble attempts to attain spirituality and face Him who hung on the tree. Put your trust in Jesus! When you take that step, His life will consume all your pain, all your rejection, and all your guilt. At that moment, for the first time in your life, the first evidence of real peace will enter into the darkened areas of your soul.

Jesus, with authority, presented a new way of spirituality. We don't have to clean up to get into the presence of the Father. We are cleansed *in* the presence of the Father. Jesus described it as a narrow way—narrow only because men refuse to believe it could be so *easy*. We think, *Surely there is some kind of sacrifice that is needed. Where's the lamb, the dove? Surely we need some kind of sacrifice. We just have to do something. Don't we?*

The road of human effort is a broad way because it is more acceptable to man's pride. Man's fallen soul wants to gain things—possessions, wealth, and even eternal life—by his own efforts. This was the sin of pride that caused the fall of the first man, and it hasn't grown any weaker since its manifestation in the garden. We are in the grip of our own dead works.

FAITH LEADS TO GRACE—GRACE GIVES HOPE FOR EXPERIENCING GLORY

Continuing his treatise to the Romans, Paul persists with his theme of grace: *...through whom also we have obtained our introduction by faith into this grace in which we stand; and we exult in hope of the glory of God* (Romans 5:2 NASB).

"But then coming under the influence of organized religion, we are seduced into continuing the journey by the performance of good works. The Apostle Paul mourned this as he watched men and women he had birthed into the Kingdom slowly returning to the old ways of religion. *After beginning with the Spirit, are you now trying to attain your goal by human effort?* (Galatians 3:3 NIV).

"Religion perpetuates this false gospel through its constant haranguing of God's people with the lash of guilt. 'You're not doing enough. Why did you miss that meeting? Why won't you teach a class?' The gospel of grace has subtly but steadily been transformed into a gospel of good works. The Church grades a person's spirituality by his church performance as opposed to his passion for a Person."[2]

Jesus came to introduce us to another way—the way of grace. The greater we grow in our experience of the powerful reality of that grace, the closer we get to the glory of God. Grace is the face of God's glory. When Moses asked to see God's glory, God told him to climb up the mountain and then He would cause His glory to pass by. The next day, while Moses was cradled in the crevice of the rocks of that ancient mountain, he felt the coming presence of God. The whole mountain shook as God's words were released into the earth. The

Grace is the face of God's glory.

meaning of God's glory was manifested in those words that vibrated in Moses' soul. *Then the LORD passed by in front of him and proclaimed, "The LORD, the LORD God, compassionate and gracious, slow to anger, and abounding in lovingkindness and truth"* (Exodus 34:6, NASB). Glory is reserved for those who have discovered this amazing grace. The glory of God is in His compassion, His grace, and His love.

Too often people overlook the importance of grace and concentrate on the good lives they live, how many scriptures they can quote, or how many times they go to church each week. But none of that will get us to heaven. It is the grace of Jesus Christ that will take us home.

We are all addicted to the Protestant work ethic. And work is a good thing. Work gets things done and provides rewards. But when it comes to the things of God, the work that really matters is the work that God has already done through His Son. The only work left for you to do is to simply say yes to what Christ has done for you. Charles Spurgeon, the prince of preachers, best described that grace with these majestic words.

"I think it well to turn a little to one side that I may ask my reader to observe adoringly the fountain-head of our salvation, which is the grace of God. 'By grace are ye saved.'

"Because God is gracious, therefore sinful men are forgiven, converted, purified, and saved. It is not because of anything in them, or that ever can be in them, that they are saved; but because of the boundless love, goodness, pity, compassion, mercy, and grace of God. Tarry a moment, then, at the well-head. Behold the pure river of water of life, as it proceeds out of the throne of God and of the Lamb!"[3]

LET'S GET BOLD!

Let us therefore draw near with confidence to the throne of grace, that we may receive mercy and may find grace to help in time of need (Hebrews 4:16 NASB). Most people don't have a prayer life because they think that God won't hear them because they've sinned. They have been mesmerized by the drumbeat of religion that insists that you must be perfect before you can enter God's presence. According to their religious decrees, God's throne is a place of judgment.

Paul upsets the proverbial religious applecart when he tells us that the throne of God is a throne of grace. Even though it is plain as day in the Scriptures, religious folk refuse to see that Jesus, by His life, paid a price so that all men could walk into the throne room of God. They are welcomed there because of what Jesus has done. By His righteousness—not by your own works—a doorway into the presence of God has been opened. It is a wide door, a love door. All you have to do is turn away from your sin (we call that repentance) and go through the door confessing your sin and believing in your heart that Jesus has already done all that needs to be done.

Get bold. Cast aside your fear and shame and walk through that door. In the presence of God, your prayers are heard, your life is changed, and God reveals His plans for your life.

Much more then, having now been justified by His blood, we shall be saved from wrath, through him (Romans 5:9 NASB). Some of you are afraid to come into God's presence because you don't think you can live up to His standards. You keep hanging around the edges of the church, but you never enter because you can't shake off the feeling of being unworthy. What you don't understand is that those people on the inside are just as unworthy as you are. So what's the difference?

How does one shake off the parasites of irrelevance and worthlessness? There is only one way. You must come to the place where once and forever you accept that there is nothing you can do. The blood of Jesus and the grace of God have made a way for you. You simply

Judgment is averted by grace.

put your faith in the grace of God, and you'll be saved from the wrath to come. Judgment is averted by grace.

God sent his dear Son to give you access. He wanted to make it that easy. He knew that you could never come through the hard way of the law. The law could never work. Jesus descended into the darkness of our disorder and provided a way to bring us back into His order. Then He simply said, "Follow Me. Follow Me into the bright lights of grace and glory."

Now, I can hear you saying, "It can't be that easy." Well, it is. It is wonderful, incredible, unbelievable, astonishing, and extraordinary *amazing* grace.

Sometimes we just don't understand what the grace of God is all about. We keep falling back into the old ways. It seems easier to trust in our works than in His work. People still don't want to trust God. They want to roll that stone back in place at the empty tomb. They say, "I've said my prayers, done my penance, paid my dues, and now I am ready to serve God." No! You must repent of all of those "dead" works. Yes, I said "dead." You must stop depending on your works and learn to accept God's grace.

THE GIFT

In the first few chapters of Paul's letters to the Romans, Paul wrestles with the issues of sin, law, grace, faith, righteousness, and life in God. As he passes through the dark night of sin, unrighteousness, wrath, and judgment, he finally arrives at the summit of grace and glory. There on the mountain, his eyes have seen the glory of the gift.

> *...being justified as a **gift** by His grace through the redemption which is in Christ Jesus.*
> —Romans 3:24 NASB

> *But the **free gift** is not like the transgression. For if by the transgression of the one the many died, much more did the grace of God and the gift by the grace of the one Man, Jesus Christ, abound to the many.*

*And the **gift** is not like that which came through the
one who sinned; for on the one hand the judgment
arose from one transgression resulting in condemnation, but on the other hand the **free gift** arose
from many transgressions resulting in justification.
For if by the transgression of the one, death reigned
through the one, much more those who receive the
abundance of grace and of the **gift** of righteousness
will reign in life through the One, Jesus Christ.*
—Romans 5:15-17 NASB

*For the wages of sin is death, but the **free gift** of
God is eternal life in Christ Jesus our Lord.*
—Romans 6:23 NASB

The Greek word for *gift* is *charisma,* and it means, "a bestow-
ment, a grant, an offer, or a free gift." To reject a gift is the height
of disgracing and dishonoring the giver. Through one man, sin
came to all men. *That was a curse.* Man was cursed by sin. But
through one Man, righteousness has
come to all men. *That is a gift.* The
law entered that the offense might
abound, that it might rule over man,
and that it might prove that no one
is able to keep the law. The law came
so you can understand your weak-

*Grace is stronger than
sin and more powerful
than the law.*

nesses and your powerlessness in the face of the ominous law.
But the Bible gives us this good news: Where sin abounded,
grace abounded more. What does that mean? It means that
grace is stronger than sin and more powerful than the law. This
makes me feel like a little kid in a toyshop! This is amazing—
amazing grace, how sweet the sound.

"What does God want?" you ask. He wants you to believe in your heart and confess with your mouth that He is Lord. If you are grateful for what He has done, you must accept the grace. What a sting it creates in the heart of God when anyone refuses this awesome gift.

> *And it happened that as He was reclining at the table in the house, behold many tax-gatherers and sinners came and were dining with Jesus and His disciples. And when the Pharisees saw this, they said to His disciples, "Why is your Teacher eating with the tax-gatherers and sinners?" But when He heard this, He said, "It is not those who are healthy who need a physician, but those who are sick. But go and learn what this means, 'I desire compassion, and not sacrifice,' for I did not come to call the righteous, but sinners."*
> —Matthew 9:10-13 NASB

The gift is more appreciated by those who know they have great needs. Those who think they are righteous have no appreciation for the gift. They see no value in the gift. But those little ones who truly understand how weak and helpless they are can be found standing on the street corner of spiritual desire, looking for a handout of amazing grace.

SQUEEZED BY LOVE

For the love of Christ controls us, having concluded this, that one died for all, therefore all died (2 Corinthians 5:14 NASB). Paul says that this amazing grace, this love of Christ, controls, squeezes, and seizes us. We are in the grip of His grace! *And he died for all, that those who live should no longer live for them-*

selves, but for Him who died for them and rose again. Therefore, from now on, we regard no one according to the flesh. Even though we have known Christ according to the flesh, yet now we know him thus no longer (2 Corinthians 5:15,16 NKJV). Paul arrived at this wonderful conclusion: Because of Christ's death, I also died. Died to what? Died to the old way of living—the way of sin, shame, guilt, and condemnation. He died. I died. His love entered my chaotic world and put me in a divine chokehold until I cried, "Uncle." I gave up when I found myself in the grip of grace—I found forgiveness, healing, cleansing, and a new way of living.

As God holds us in His grip, so we also should hold others in that same grip of love. The church should have the ability to forgive and walk in love towards one another. We are all in the same grip of God's love. We are all covered with the same blood of the precious Lamb of God. Paul Tillich put it this way: "In the light of this grace we perceive the power of grace in our relations to others and to ourselves. We experience the grace of being able to look frankly into the eyes of another, the miraculous grace of reunion of life with life…We experience the grace of being able to accept the life of another, even if it be hostile and harmless to us, for, through grace, we know that it belongs to the same Ground to which we belong, and by which we have been accepted."[4]

God says He sent Jesus to be a covering for you so that when God sniffs the air around you, He smells the sweet incense of His Son. I can remember when I used to feel that God wouldn't hear my prayers if there was something wrong with me. If I felt a little depressed, then it must be that God hated me. My moods affected my perception of God's feelings towards me. But a day came when I was finally gripped by the grace of God. When you get in the clutches of compassion, you know that you are welcomed in His presence. I know that God continues to cover me until He can heal me. I know that I am in the palm of His hand. Why would you reject His grace that is reaching out to you? Why would you seek to go another way? Why would you try to go it alone? Let yourself be captured by His compassion and locked in His love!

RECONCILING THE RECORDS

Now all these things are from God, who reconciled us to Himself through Christ, and gave us the ministry of reconciliation (2 Corinthians 5:18, NASV). This verse means that I must tell others about the good news. Evangelism is a scary thing to most people. They could never imagine themselves knocking on doors or standing on a street corner passing out gospel tracts. Well, here's the deal. Maybe you don't have to do that. Maybe you just have to care for those lives that cross your path every day. Maybe you need new eyes for the invisible so that you can see their desperate need for this amazing grace. Sometimes we tend to see the unsaved as the enemy who is out to crush us somehow, rather than just plain people who would gladly welcome a cup of water to quench their thirsting souls. Don't give them religion; give them grace, give them Jesus. Tell them what He has done for you. Those who are in the grip of this amazing grace have a powerful message for the world. It is the message that the modern world needs. It is a world of the isolated and lonely who are looking for a little love. We pass them by every day and miss the opportunity of offering that helping hand.

Those who are in the grip of this amazing grace have a powerful message for the world.

Second Corinthians 5:19 says, ...*namely, that God was in Christ reconciling the world to Himself, not counting their trespasses against them, and He has committed to us the word of reconciliation* (NASB). When tax time comes around, and it is time to make sure all your records are correct, you call for an audit. An accountant then reconciles your books. You make sure that every expense was entered correctly and that every debt was paid accordingly. Thus, everything is now reconciled.

God was in Christ making sure that everything came out right. Christ looked at your debit line and balanced it with His life. Your debt was beyond your means to pay. You were living in sin, way beyond your means. Debt was piling up. You had maxed out the credit cards of sin and were facing the consequences of your actions. Jesus entered into your life and put His life on the line. He walked the line for you and covered all your debt, saying, "I'm not going to hold it against you in Christ." Now, if you think I'm just giving you a license to sin, I'm not. Grace is not a license to sin; it is a power to live in a way that you never knew could be possible.

I am telling you that Jesus saved your life. This is what we call the doctrine of Soteria. But it is much more than a concept, a principle, a doctrine, or a theology. It is a spiritual reality. Jesus saved you, rescued you, and salvaged your life. He bailed you out and resuscitated you. This is your entrance into the kingdom of God, and it is that easy. Some of you don't understand grace, and that's why you think you can't receive the Holy Ghost, a prayer language, and operate in the gifts of the Spirit. But Paul said that having begun in the Spirit, we have this tendency, this lapse of memory, and we go back to the flesh. We get in the door by grace, but once we get in, we tend to go back to that old "works" thing!

Everything God gives you is by grace and not by your own merit. You think, "God won't hear my prayers because they are not holy enough." No! "Well, I just need more faith." Even the faith you have is a gift. When you have faith, you have favor in the grace of God—a faith that is focused on His ability, not your ability.

When you have faith, you have favor in the grace of God—a faith that is focused on His ability, not your ability.

I can see lights going off in your head. "Oh, my God. Thank God it's up to Him." When you really get this, then you will enter into a spiritual freedom that you have never known. No more fear of going into His presence.

Second Corinthians 5:20,21 goes on to say, *Therefore, we are ambassadors for Christ, as though God were entreating through us; we beg you on behalf of Christ, be reconciled to God. He made Him who knew no sin to be sin on our behalf, that we might become the righteousness of God in Him* (NASB). Are you getting the picture? When you were in a mess and did not have a clue how to get out of it, someone was cleaning up your mess. When you couldn't find your way to God, He found His way to you. When you were so miserable and lost, God came into your life and rearranged the living room of your heart, cleaning out all of that excess furniture of guilt, shame, and condemnation.

Second Corinthians 6:1 declares, *And working together with Him, we also urge you not to receive the grace of God in vain* (NASB). In other words, don't say this is good news and then return back to the old ways of "I owe, I owe. It's off to work I go." Don't sing that tune. Continue to swim in the ocean of that amazing grace. Continue to live your life according to what God has done for you.

A REVIEW OF THE GOOD NEWS

1. While you were a sinner, not caring about God or His purposes for your life, Christ came and got you out of hot water and settled your debt.

2. The only way to experience what God has done is to simply accept it. Turn your back on trying to do it your way and recognize that all things will come to those who simply trust in Him.

3. All the spiritual riches we need are in Christ, and we have access to them through Calvary. We can enter the door that leads to great treasures. The key to that door is what Christ did on the cross.

4. The message of grace is good news. It's amazing grace. It is blessed assurance. And you get to tell others. How could you not tell somebody? This is just too good to keep to yourself.

5. The church is to be a place where people can experience that grace. Paul spent a lot of time talking about grace and about the church. These two go together. The church is not really the church if there is no grace, and grace needs a place where it can manifest itself. Why are so many people leaving the church and why are so few people attracted to the church? The answer is simple. We have lost our message. We have allowed our image to be corrupted. We are more of a house of judgment than of grace. If we get our message back and allow the Spirit of God to give the church an *extreme makeover* then people will flood into the house of God.

A FINAL LOOK AT THE PORTRAIT OF GRACE

Grace is found in a garden and on a tree. In a garden, Jesus wrestled with the task that was before Him. He was tempted to draw back, but in the agony of the moment, He responded, "Not my

will, but Yours." Grace was extended to us that day when Jesus said yes to His Father. He was dragged out of the garden by religious men and taken to the tree. On the tree, the full extent of His amazing grace was manifested to the whole world. The

Grace was extended to us that day when Jesus said yes to His Father.

prophet Isaiah drew a powerful picture in chapter 53 of his book. It is a portrayal of agony and pain.

> *For he shall grow up before him as a tender plant, and as a root out of a dry ground: he hath no form nor comeliness; and when we shall see him, there is no beauty that we should desire him. He is despised and rejected of men; a man of sorrows, and acquainted with grief: and we hid as it were our faces from him; he was despised, and we esteemed him not. Surely he hath borne our griefs, and carried our sorrows: yet we did esteem him stricken, smitten of God, and afflicted. But he was wounded for our transgressions, he was bruised for our iniquities: the chastisement of our peace was upon him; and with his stripes we are healed. All we like sheep have gone astray; we have turned every one to his own way; and the LORD hath laid on him the iniquity of us all. He was oppressed, and he was afflicted, yet he opened not his mouth: he is brought as a lamb to the slaughter, and as a sheep*

before her shearers is dumb, so he openeth not his mouth.

—Isaiah 53:2-7

God paid a price for you that you couldn't pay. He put down the deposit to rescue you, and then He opened a door to eternal life for you. When you couldn't do it, He went ahead and put the guarantee down through His Son. The stripes on His back were for you. His blood cries out for God's healing power in your life. This is about love...about His love for you. Do you get it? Most of us don't because we have placed such a low value on what He has done and who we are. But it is my prayer that God will open your eyes to see the value of that amazing grace and the deep love that He has for you. Religion was never about procedures; it was always about passion.

In closing this chapter, I want to press this issue home with a closing thought on Calvary. Someone once said that repetition is the mother of learning. We don't always get the message the first time. Since we have lived so long under the illusion that "it's all about me," we have to keep pounding the message home until light dawns and we fully understand that "it's all about Him."

8 THINGS ABOUT CALVARY

1. **(Mark 14:32-42)** *In the face of His coming death, Jesus overcame the "fear factor."* Fear is a formidable foe of mankind, and Jesus faced it head-on, giving us the courage to do the same.

2. **(Mark 14:65)** *Jesus bore our shame.* He was spit on and struck, and people ridiculed Him, yelling out at Him to prophesy. What shame was laid on Him! He who was once

in the glorious presence of the Father was rejected and humiliated by the very ones He came to rescue. But Jesus defeated shame, and because He is righteous, He will defeat your shame.

3. **(Mark 15:17)** *Jesus took our pain and set us free.* The crown of thorns was forced on His head, and as a result, great drops of blood came pouring down His face. His head was pierced with pain so that your head could be delivered and renewed from all the nagging thoughts of an old, guilt-ridden, lust-filled, and damaged mind. Oh, my God, it is amazing! He did all of this for you and me.

4. **(Mark 15:15)** *Jesus was scourged and beaten.* I am sure that many of you remember that horrific scene from the movie, *The Passion of the Christ.* If you are like me, it is burned into your memory. How could we forget the pain and agony He endured? He did not deserve this treacherous beating, yet He did it for us.

5. **(Mark 15:19)** *The Roman soldiers mocked Jesus.* They made fun of Him, and sarcastically reminded Him that He was supposed to be the King and Lord. They ridiculed His authority and His personage. The devil was laughing, thinking that what he could not get in the desert, he would get at the cross—getting rid of this man forever. But the devil's plan and man's actions played right into God's hands. The devil couldn't see that what he planned for the Son of God ended up being a great victory for heaven—and for you and me. The authority that was mocked became the authority that would rule the world.

The authority that was mocked became the authority that would rule the world.

Aimee Simple McPherson talked about the four-square gospel. She said that Jesus is our salvation, He is our savior, He is our deliverer, and He is our soon-coming King. The wounded Savior will be the coming King.

6. **(Psalm 22:16) Jesus cancelled our debt of sin.** Paul wrote these words to the church at Colossae ...*having canceled out the certificate of debt consisting of decrees against us and which was hostile to us; and He has taken it out of the way, having nailed it to the cross* (Colossians 2:14 NASB). With each thud of the hammer driving the nails into His hands and feet, Jesus cancelled out every accusation against you. Every dirty rotten thing that was held against you was nailed to that tree with Him. Everything that made you feel unworthy was taken away. All the debts racked up by a life of sin are cancelled out and rendered void by the nails in His hands and feet.

7. **(John 19:34) Jesus' side was pierced with a spear**, and immediately blood and water came out. As we have already seen in the book of Romans, Jesus was the second Adam. The first man was Adam, and from his side came a woman, named Eve. Out of Jesus' side came blood and water—the bride of the Lamb was washed with His blood and the water of the Spirit.

   Adam's side brought forth the human race; Jesus' side brought a divine race. Jesus' death, burial, and resurrection brought forth a new breed of men and women. He gave birth to the church of the living God, redeemed by the blood of the Lamb. As Paul said, "You were bought with a price." You could not pay the bill, so Jesus picked up the tab.

8. **(Luke 23:34-35) Those gathered around the cross divided Jesus' garments and cast lots for them.** Jesus, looking down

on this pathetic scene, simply said, "Forgive them Father." He let them take His garments. He was made naked so that you could be clothed. He was stripped of His dignity so that you could be wrapped in a cloak of nobility.

Finally, the end came—He breathed His last breath and the Spirit left Him. At that very moment, the deal was done. Satan was defeated, and the curse of the law on your life was overruled. When He died, you died with Him. When He said it is finished, it was finished. You were then planted with Him in His death, and then on that Resurrection morning, when He arose, you rose with Him. You are now seated in heavenly places. This is what's so amazing about grace.

You can't find a better deal. "What do I need to do?" you ask. You need to believe in your heart, and confess with your mouth that Jesus is Lord. You need to say, "Lord God, I place my hope in Your marvelous grace."

The tomb is empty. Religion tries to put Jesus back in the tomb, but it won't work. He has already ascended to His Father, and we are now seated with Him.

This makes me want to worship Him, breaking out in a song of praise to my wonderful Lord. It doesn't make me want to pull back from Him in fear. It makes me want to run to Him and thank Him for all that He has done for me.

I spent many years in church, trying and trying to do things right, but I always felt like it was never enough. What a day it was when love opened up the door to my heart, and I was introduced to the amazing grace of God. It was on that day that I first understood that it's not about me; it's about Him.

In Deuteronomy 28, we read about the blessing that grace has delivered to us:

Blessed shall you be in the city, and blessed shall you be in the country. Blessed shall be the fruit of your body, the produce of your ground, and the increase of your herds, the increase of your cattle and the offspring of your flocks. Blessed shall be your basket and your kneading bowl. Blessed shall you be when you come in, and blessed shall you be when you go out. The Lord will cause your enemies who rise against you to be defeated before your face; they shall come out against you one way and flee before you seven ways.

—Deuteronomy 28:3-7 NKJV

THIS IS AMAZING GRACE!

The Lord will command the blessing to come upon your life, and all that you set your hand to do, He will bless. The Lord will establish you as a holy people to himself.

The Lord will open to you His good treasure, the heavens, and you will be blessed with His favor. He will cause the rain of spiritual renewal to pour down upon you, and He will bless all the work of your hands. You will be a lender and not a borrower. The Lord will make you the head and not the tail. You will be above only and not beneath.

Then all the people on the earth will see that you are called by the name of the Lord, and they will desire what you have. In that day, men will see the great grace of God upon His people, and will come back to the house of the Lord.

This is what is so amazing about His grace!

Grace
IN ACTION

*God, being rich in mercy, because of His great love
with which He loved us, even when we were dead
in our transgressions, made us alive together with
Christ (by grace you have been saved), and raised
us up with Him, and seated us with Him in the
heavenly places, in Christ Jesus, in order that in the
ages to come He might show the surpassing riches of
His grace in kindness toward us in Christ Jesus. For
by grace you have been saved through faith; and
that not of yourselves, it is the gift of God; not as a
result of works, that no one should boast."*

—Ephesians 2:1-9 NASB

What a wonderful gift God has given you through His Son.
This is unmerited favor—you get what you don't deserve. It
seems too good to be true, but God loved you enough to give
you this amazing grace. Don't forget that Jesus paid the ultimate price that you might enjoy the ultimate life. Discover
His amazing grace, and spend time with the giver of this gift,
acknowledging your deep love and appreciation for what He
has done for you. Determine that you will always remember
what is so amazing about His grace and forever remain in the
grip of that grace.

CHAPTER THREE

THE WORKINGS OF GRACE

But by the grace of God I am what I am: and his grace which was bestowed upon me was not in vain; but I laboured more abundantly than they all: yet not I, but the grace of God which was with me.
— 1 Corinthians 15:10

HE MESSAGE OF GRACE IS A SCANDAL TO THOSE who have chosen to live their lives within the fence of rules and regulations. If we are not careful, Old Testament law can quickly be transformed into a seductive New Testament law. Grace is the good news sent to us

*Grace is the good news
sent to us from the
printing presses of heaven.*

from the printing presses of heaven. I have meticulously and repetitively tried to present to you the fact that grace is based on what God has done, not what you can do. In this chapter, we will turn the corner and view the grace of God from a different angle.

Although grace is not dependent on your works, it does not mean that you do not work. That is a subversion of the message of grace.

We have to walk a narrow line as we seek to hold two truths in perfect tension. On the one hand, you do not work to get His grace, but on the other hand, when you have His grace you will work. As followers of the Lord, we must hold these truths in harmony so there is no discord in our lives. The workings of grace is an occupational force, manufacturing the plans and purposes of God through our lives.

THE OPERATION OF DIVINE GRACE

It is a foundational truth of the New Testament that we get nothing in life without the force of God's grace working in our lives. As Paul said, "I am what I am by the grace of God." All that we are and all that we do are based upon the operation of divine grace in our lives. This is powerfully confirmed in the writings of Paul, the man who was obsessed with God's grace.

> *Having then gifts differing according to the grace
> that is given to us, whether prophecy, let us prophesy
> according to the proportion of faith.*
> —Romans 12:6

*According to the grace of God which is given unto
me, as a wise masterbuilder, I have laid the foundation, and another buildeth thereon. But let every
man take heed how he buildeth thereupon.*

—1 Corinthians 3:10

*And God is able to make all grace abound toward
you; that ye, always having all sufficiency in all
things, may abound to every good work.*

—2 Corinthians 9:8

*To the praise of the glory of his grace, wherein he
hath made us accepted in the beloved. In whom we
have redemption through his blood, the forgiveness
of sins, according to the riches of his grace.*

—Ephesians 1:6,7

*Whereof I was made a minister, according to the
gift of the grace of God given unto me by the effec-
tual working of his power. Unto me, who am less
than the least of all saints, is this grace given, that I
should preach among the Gentiles the unsearchable
riches of Christ.*

—Ephesians 3:7,8

*But unto every one of us is given grace according to
the measure of the gift of Christ.*

—Ephesians 4:7

*Let us therefore come boldly unto the throne of
grace, that we may obtain mercy, and find grace to
help in time of need.*

—Hebrews 4:16

Wherefore we receiving a kingdom which cannot be moved, let us have grace, whereby we may serve God acceptably with reverence and godly fear.
—Hebrews 12:28

Salvation, gifts of the Spirit, character, power, strength in times of trial, service to God—all of this spiritual activity in our lives is a result of the flow of grace in and through our lives.

Grace is a river, and it must flow to us and through us.

You see, grace is a river, and it must flow *to* us and *through* us. If it gets stopped up and does not flow to others, then that grace will become stagnant and cause our lives to putrefy into selfish behavior.

I AM WHAT I AM BY THE GRACE OF GOD

Moreover, brethren, I declare unto you the gospel which I preached unto you, which also ye have received, and wherein ye stand; by which also ye are saved, if ye keep in memory what I preached unto you, unless ye have believed in vain. For I delivered unto you first of all that which I also received, how that Christ died for our sins according to the scriptures; and that he was buried, and that he rose again the third day according to the scriptures: and that he was seen of Cephas, then of the twelve: After that, he was seen of above five hundred brethren at once; of whom the greater part remain unto this present, but some are fallen asleep. After that, he was seen of James; then of all the apostles. And last of all he was seen of me also, as of one born out of due time. For I am the least of the apostles, that am not meet to be called an apostle, because I persecuted the church of God. But by the grace of God I am what I am: and his grace which was bestowed upon me was not in vain; but I laboured more abundantly than they all: yet not I, but the grace of God which was with me.

—1 Corinthians 15:1-10

Grace is not a dormant power. Grace is active, energetic, dynamic, forceful, and progressive. Grace works. Grace has a power and a motion to it. According to the grace of God, that is the rhythm and rhyme, the pace and poetry of grace. Paul said that because of the grace of God in him, he labored more abundantly. What Paul means is that because of the springs of grace emanating from his life, he was able to effectively labor on behalf of God. There was an energy within him that possessed him; it energized him so that he could do the works of God. He was once opposed to the works of God. He was once an enemy of the cross, but on that day when he met Christ, the heavens opened up and grace began to flow into his life. Paul was not working to be righteous; he was working because he became righteous by the grace that was at work within him.

Maurice Goguel, the French theologian, put it this way, "The man who is pardoned by God, that is to say, the man who has experienced the Love of God, will love Him, and will therefore be capable of being inspired by His nature. This reverses the apparently normal and rational order of the relation between religion and moralism. Usually the faithful can only enter into contact with divinity if their hearts are pure. The nearer one is to holiness the nearer to God. In the thought of Jesus, on the contrary, the communion with God which is given with the pardon of sin is the principle of the moral life and its starting point."[1]

THE TRANSFERENCE OF GRACE

No matter what you're going through, where you are, or what's happening in your life, there is a grace on the inside of you that is sufficient for everything you need in life. Not only that, there is a grace inside of you that can be transferred to others. There is a grace within you that, when released, has the power to encourage others in their melancholy moments, heal people in periods of pain, direct them in their times of confusion, and support them in their stretches of weakness.

There is a grace within you that, when released, has the power to encourage others.

I think you know what I am talking about. All of us at one time in our lives have experienced the joy of someone who crossed our path right at the opportune moment. Their presence and their words lifted us up and gave us strength to get back on the journey. We experienced the workings of grace through them.

You have experienced that "unction" of the Holy Spirit when He came upon you and gave you just the right words to speak to someone who was struggling in life and just didn't know what to do or where to turn. There's a grace inside of you that works for you, and it will work for others. This is the cadence of grace as it moves in harmony with the love of God that is seeking to make music in other people's lives through the song being sung in your life.

OBJECTIONS TO GRACE

In order to move forward in proclaiming this message of grace, we must confront some of the resistance or objections to that message of grace.

Objection #1—If you teach grace, it's going to give people a license to sin. Here's the truth about that argument. If people are going to sin, they don't need a license. They will sin with or without it. They are controlled by the power of sin, and have never really experienced the grace of God. Paul predicted this argument, and then counteracted it with these words in the letter to the Romans. *What shall we say then? Shall we continue in sin, that grace may abound? God forbid. How shall we, that are dead to sin, live any longer therein?* (Romans 6:1,2).

Objection #2—If you teach grace, it will lower the standards of the church. Again, this is an objection offered by those who do not understand the message of grace. They presuppose that grace leads to lawlessness. But this is not true. Grace does not take you down a road that will lead to a lawless lifestyle. It is just the opposite. Those who encounter grace discover a power to change their lives.

Objection #3—If you teach grace, it will deceive God's people about judgment day. Just read the writings of Paul, and you will see that it is permeated with the message of grace, but it does not water down the fact that there will be a day when we all stand before God and give an account of our actions.

Objection #4—If you teach grace, it will lead people to think they don't need to go to church. Again, if people have it in their hearts that they don't need the church, then the message of grace is not the problem. The problem is their understanding of the purpose of the church, not their misunderstanding of grace. Paul makes it clear that grace is for life in the church. Grace empowers us and gifts us in a way that we can serve one another, and that is what church is about.

UNDERSTANDING THE GRACE OF GOD

Paul said, "Because of the grace of God I labor more abundantly." What does that mean? The first thing in overcoming these objections is that you must come to a place where you have a revelation of the grace of God. When you receive a revelation of the radical and scandalous nature of the grace of God, it will rearrange everything that you have ever thought about the Christian life. Many of us have been feeding at the trough of bad news—the bad news of religion that seeks to manipulate us

Freely you have received, so freely give.

into action through the force of guilt and condemnation. The message of grace will free us from the addiction to self-servitude and release us into the service of others. This is the message of Jesus and this is the message of grace. You are now able to release to others the grace you have received. Freely you have received, so freely give.

We should never minimize the power of grace. Remember Paul's words, *Or do you think lightly of the riches of His kindness and forbearance and patience, not knowing that the kindness of God leads you to repentance?* (Romans 2:4 NASB). The message of grace teaches that God will accept you just like you are. He will receive you in the beloved. He will call you as one of His own. He will give you an inheritance of His kingdom. You have been seated with Christ in heavenly places and set in a place of glory, honor, and riches through the spirit of grace.

Grace teaches us that God starts on the inside of us. He says He will keep working in us and complete that work according to the grace that works in us. Paul Tillich powerfully described the force of grace in this way: "Grace is the reunion of life with life, the reconciliation of the self with itself. Grace is the acceptance of that which is rejected. Grace transforms fate into a meaningless destiny; it changes guilt into confidence and courage. There is something triumphant in the word 'grace': in spite of the abounding of sin grace abounds much more."[2]

Now unto him that is able to do exceeding abundantly above all that we ask or think, according to the power that worketh in us (Ephesians 3:20). Grace says you have been called, reconciled, accepted, saved, healed, and delivered. All of this is in agreement with the power that works within us. In his letter to the Philippians, Paul goes on to say, *Being confident of this very thing, that he which hath begun a good work in you will perform it until the day of Jesus Christ* (Philippians 1:6). We look at our daily lives, and we don't think that anything is happening within us. You will never see your change by looking at your life from day to day. You can only see this work by looking back over time. Grace is at work regardless of whether you see it or feel it. It is working to change your attitudes, your hurts, and your weaknesses. Grace is involved in a great reconstruction project as it continues to change you.

For it is God which worketh in you both to will and to do of his good pleasure (Philippians 2:13). The Holy Spirit, by the power of grace, is working in you. He is creating desire, power, and longing so that you will want to and be able to do the work that God has planned for your life.

And the very God of peace sanctify you wholly; and I pray God your whole spirit and soul and body be preserved blameless unto the coming of our Lord Jesus Christ. Faithful is he that calleth you, who also will do it (1 Thessalonians 5:23,24). He who calls you is faithful, and He also will do it. We are talking about grace—about the workings of grace. We are talking about an internal energy that is at work within you. The Holy Spirit puts a lasso on your life, roping you into His purposes for your life. The Holy Spirit knows how to keep you on course when

everybody else is against your course. He knows how to keep you on course when you don't even know what or where your course is anymore!

GUIDELINES FOR GRACE

Guideline #1—The simplicity of this grace is something that you just need to receive. No sweat and no workaholics are allowed to enter this door. Grace comes to those who know they need it and are willing to simply accept from God's hand what they need. Now, I know this is a blow to the pride of those who think that surely there is something they must do. Well, if you insist on doing something, then just trust Him. Allow your faith (which is really not yours…it is a gift) to receive what has already been deposited in your bank account. That's why Romans 8:26 says, *Likewise the Spirit also helpeth our infirmities: for we know not what we should pray for as we ought: but the Spirit itself maketh intercession for us with groanings which cannot be uttered.* You have always needed help. You just didn't know it. There is an old adage that says, "God helps those who help themselves." That has been repeated so often that most people believe it is a Bible verse, but it is not in the Bible. It comes under the topic of "bad teaching." God helps us because we can't help ourselves!

"Well, I can't pray because God sees me as being unfit to pray," you may say. Hey, that's the whole idea about prayer. You come to Him because you are unfit, unworthy, and weak. You come to Him so that He can help you. He sends the Holy Spirit who knows where you need to go. The Holy Spirit knows what direction you need to take, and He knows the information you need along the way. He knows how to shut you up when you need to shut up and how to get you to speak up when you need to speak up! He knows, and you don't know. That's why you need to approach the one who does know.

Guideline #2—*The next step is to repent from dead works.* That is one of the foundational principles of Hebrews 6. Which works are those? Well, they are all those works that you do out of your own flesh, effort, and apart from the grace of God. They are dead, useless, and not able to accomplish what God wants in your life. Good works come from lives that are allowing God's grace to flow to them. Good works come from the grace of God working on the inside of you. You're never going to do a work that is approved by God unless it's by His Spirit working in you. And you know what? God's grace and anointing in you are willing

Good works come from the grace of God working on the inside of you.

and able to make you a true servant of God. Your works become dead when you don't allow grace to flow like a river through you. Don't dam it up with unbelief, selfishness, and pride.

Guideline #3—*You have to let grace flow through you to others.* Grace must flow. That is the nature of grace. When grace stops, it loses its power and potential. Keep it flowing by giving it away. Grace is like anointing. It is not to make you famous; it is to help you serve other people. Jesus established that principle in the Upper Room. As He washed the disciples' feet, He was illustrating to them the power of the towel. Grace flows to you so that you are empowered to wash other people's feet. If your faith is based on who He is, then you don't have to worry about how much faith you have. You just need to have enough faith to believe that He is able to do what He said He would do and that He is who He says He is. Just let that grace flow.

WALK WORTHY OF YOUR CALLING

I therefore, the prisoner of the Lord, beseech you that ye walk worthy of the vocation wherewith ye are called (Ephesians 4:1). In the light of this wonderful gift, what can you do in response? You can walk in a way that is worthy of the calling that is on your life. Walk worthy of this grace that has been deposited into your life. The only way you can walk it out is according to His grace that He put within you. All He is asking you to do is to let His Spirit touch your spirit, and then the call can become a reality.

His grace leads us to a place that is worthy of who He is and makes us worthy of the call that He has placed on us. You can make Him proud. The message of grace does not forfeit the message of repentance. A worthy walk is a repentant walk. Repentance simply means turning around and walking in a new direction. Repentance *always* precedes deliverance. And God said that His goodness will not leave you like you are. It's going to get you out of bed and set you on your course. Repentance means being convinced that the direction you have taken for your life is a wrong direction. It doesn't mean beating yourself up, condemning yourself, and doing all kinds of penance. It simply means to turn away. He's pushing one way, and you're pulling another way. Since God is stronger than you are, you need to give up and let grace have its work in you.

Give up and let grace have its work in you.

Religious folks can talk about it, and religious preachers can preach about it, but no one will do it until they become convinced of the grace of God. Evangelism, prayer, following God—all of these are issues we struggle with until we have an encounter with God's grace. Then evangelism is no longer a problem. Prayer becomes a pleasure. The Christian walk is a joy. And grace makes the difference.

GRACE AND MINISTRY

> *For I say, through the grace given unto me, to every man that is among you, not to think of himself more highly than he ought to think; but to think soberly, according as God hath dealt to every man the measure of faith. For as we have many members in one body, and all members have not the same office: so we, being many, are one body in Christ, and every one members one of another. Having then gifts differing according to the grace that is given to us, whether prophecy, let us prophesy according to the proportion of faith; or ministry, let us wait on our ministering: or he that teacheth, on teaching; or he that exhorteth, on exhortation: he that giveth, let him do it with simplicity; he that ruleth, with diligence; he that sheweth mercy, with cheerfulness.*
> —Romans 12:3-8

Having gifts differing according to the grace that is given to us determines our place in the body of Christ. It is not our ingenuity, strength, wisdom, or education. The determining factor is the grace factor. Grace is a river, but it is also a light that is refracted through a prism. The colors of light that are manifested in other people's lives are determined by how grace interacts with our nature. God created all of us in a very unique way, and the portion of grace we have received displays that distinctiveness.

Some people receive grace in a way that motivates them in the area of the prophetic word. Others receive grace, and it is manifested in a gracious and giving spirit. Still others receive grace and become encouragers in the body of Christ. We have all been given a portion of grace, so let us use it in ministering to others.

Paul goes on to say that this grace, generally speaking, is manifested in how the body of Christ responds to one another.

> *Let love be without hypocrisy. Abhor what is evil. Cling to what is good. Be kindly affectionate to one another with brotherly love, in honor giving preference to one another, not lacking in diligence, fervent in spirit, serving the Lord; rejoicing in hope, patient in tribulation, continuing steadfastly in prayer, distributing to the needs of the saints, given to hospitality. Bless those who persecute you; bless and do not curse. Rejoice with those who rejoice, and weep with those who weep. Be of the same mind toward one another. Do not set your mind on high things, but associate with the humble.*
> —Roman 12:9-16 NKJV

This is the power and dynamics of grace as it operates in the body of Christ. This is the church at its best. This is the witness that will attract the world to seek what we have discovered.

Grace changes your life and gives you power. But grace also gifts you to serve others in the strength that has been given to you by the grace of God. The grace we have received is not only for our benefit but also for the benefit of the whole church. There is an anointing, a grace or power, that is working in you to perform the work of Christ.

It is the work of Jesus among us. Jesus ministers to His people through the grace that is flowing through His children.

You are anointed and appointed. You have a calling that is based on the grace that has been given to you.

You have a calling that is based on the grace that has been given to you.

Every one of you has a gift that comes by grace. Just trust the gift-giver. You may not feel like you have anything you can say or do—but you do. You just haven't discovered the reservoir of grace that resides within you. It has been dammed up far too long. By the power of the Spirit, that dam can be broken—then grace will flow and you will be amazed at the words He will give you, the power that will be yours, and the gifts that will operate through you.

When the grace of God is working in your life, everybody sees it and knows it. It just works. If you trust Him, He'll give you the "will" and the "power" to work for His good pleasure. When you begin to activate the grace of God, He says, "I guarantee that I will complete what I began in you." If you will just keep grace running through your body, then your life will become complete, and ministry will flow to others!

GRACE AND THE DAY OF SMALL BEGINNINGS

And the angel of the LORD protested unto Joshua, saying, Thus saith the LORD of hosts; If thou wilt walk in my ways, and if thou wilt keep my charge, then thou shalt also judge my house, and shalt also keep my courts, and I will give thee places to walk among these that stand by. Hear now, O Joshua the high priest, thou, and thy fellows that sit before thee: for they are men wondered at: for, behold, I will bring forth my servant the BRANCH. For behold the stone that I have laid before Joshua; upon one stone shall be seven eyes: behold, I will engrave the graving thereof, saith the LORD of hosts, and I will remove the iniquity of that land in one day. In that day, saith the LORD of hosts, shall ye call every man his neighbour under the vine and under the fig tree.

—Zechariah 3:6-10

Grace gives you eyes to see the invisible, the things that others do not see. God will let you see all kinds of things if

Grace gives you eyes to see the invisible, the things that others do not see.

you're willing to look through the eyes of grace. Unfortunately, most of us look at life through our grief, rather than through His grace. Grace has to heal our pain before we get those kinds of spiritual eyes.

Through the eyes of grace, Joshua was able to take a peek into the other world and hear things that he had never heard. Remember, grace always works. Grace helps you see things that others cannot see.

Joshua heard such amazing things. He heard promises that were beyond his ability to fulfill—promises that would be his if he simply walked with God. Joshua received eyes to see the future and what God was going to do. What had become a way of life for Joshua should be a way of life for us.

And the angel that talked with me came again, and waked me, as a man that is wakened out of his sleep, and said unto me, What seest thou? And I said, I have looked, and behold a candlestick all of gold, with a bowl upon the top of it, and his seven lamps thereon, and seven pipes to the seven lamps, which are upon the top thereof: and two olive trees by it, one upon the right side of the bowl, and the other upon the left side thereof. So I answered and spake to the angel that talked with me, saying, What are these, my lord? Then the angel that talked with me answered and said unto me, Knowest thou not what these be? And I said, No, my lord. Then he answered and spake unto me, saying, This is the word of the Lord unto Zerubbabel, saying, Not by might, nor by power, but by my spirit, saith the Lord of hosts. Who art thou, O great mountain? before Zerubbabel thou shalt become a plain: and he shall bring forth the headstone thereof with shoutings, crying, **Grace, grace unto it.** *Moreover the word of the Lord came unto me, saying, The hands of Zerubbabel have laid the foundation of this house; his hands shall also finish it; and thou shalt know that the Lord of hosts hath sent me unto you. For who hath despised the day of small things? For they shall rejoice, and shall see the plummet in the hand of Zerubbabel with those seven; they are the eyes of the Lord, which run to and fro through the whole earth. Then answered I, and said unto him, What are these two olive trees upon the right side of the candlestick and upon the left side thereof? And I answered again, and said unto him, What be these two olive branches which through the two golden pipes empty the golden oil out of themselves? And he answered me and said, Knowest thou not what these be? And I said, No, my lord. Then said he, These are the two anointed ones, that stand by the Lord of the whole earth.*

—Zechariah 4:1-14

Who is despising the day of small things? Who does not understand the *grace* that should be shouted to that mountain, and who does not understand that in the Spirit, man will cause that mountain to be removed? Who does not understand how God is working it *in* you and *through* you and that it's not by your own strength? It's not by your own intellect, and it's not by your own ability to conjure up some manmade response to your troubles. *Not by might, nor by power, but by my spirit, saith the* LORD. So don't despise the day of small things. God loves to start small in ways that men do not see, and then when He has completed His task, all will be surprised at what the Lord has done.

The two anointed ones are standing to work on your behalf—the Spirit and the Word. This is the *Word* of the Lord. *Not by might, nor by power, but by my spirit.* Now you have the spirit of grace working on the inside of you. The two anointed ones will take the despised day of small beginnings and transform them into a mountain of glory in your life.

You must look at the mountain of pain, trouble, and difficulty that is before you and shout out loud, "Grace, grace to those mountains!" What God has started in your life, He will complete. He not only will give you the *will,* but He will give you the *ability* to do it.

GOOD WORKS

But in a great house there are not only vessels of gold and silver, but also of wood and clay, some for honor and some for dishonor (2 Timothy 2:20 NKJV). In God's house, everything has value. Everything has its function when it is used in the way it was designed. Once you find your value, then you will be able to bring glory to God. When you allow the grace of God to fill your vessel, then it will become a vessel of honor.

For we are His workmanship, created in Christ Jesus for good works, which God prepared beforehand, that we should walk in them (Ephesians 2:10 NKJV). God has designed your life in such a way that it has the potential of producing good works. When you turn from the dead works

When you allow the grace of God to fill your vessel, then it will become a vessel of honor.

of religion, then you open up the possibility that your life will be filled with good works. Grace creates the possibility for those good works.

Resident on the inside of you right now is the fire of God, the power of God, the strength of God, the worth of God, and the greatness of God. He's working to do something in you. God's grace is at work within you, and because of that grace, you can do something that nobody else can do. The grace of God won't let you give up! About the time you think you will give up, there He is, getting you back up again. You think that you are chasing God, but the truth of the matter is that He is chasing you. This is grace at work.

Grace
IN ACTION

As each one has received a gift, minister it to one another, as good stewards of the manifold grace of God. If anyone speaks, let him speak as the oracles of God. If anyone ministers, let him do it as with the ability which God supplies, that in all things God may be glorified through Jesus Christ, to whom belong the glory and the dominion forever and ever.

—1 Peter 4:10,11 NKJV

Everything you are and everything you have are the result of the wonderful gift of God. Freely you have received His magnificent grace, and freely you must give it to others. Actually, the only way you can keep that grace flowing in your own life is by giving it away…transferring it to others.

Recognize that you don't work to become righteous—you are righteous by the grace that works in you. Ask God to create in you the desire to do the work He has planned for your life. Then allow His grace to empower and gift you in ways that allow you to find ways to serve others.

CHAPTER FOUR

THE POWER OF GRACE

...the man Christ Jesus...gave Himself a ransom for all...

—1 Timothy 2:6 NKJV

THE SIMPLEST AND MOST PROFOUND ASPECT OF Christianity is found in the death, burial, and resurrection of Jesus Christ. It was upon the cross that He died as a sacrifice. All areas of human existence were provided for by grace through faith in Jesus Christ.

*Surely he hath borne our griefs, and carried our
sorrows: yet we did esteem him stricken, smitten
of God, and afflicted. But he was wounded for our
transgressions, he was bruised for our iniquities: the
chastisement of our peace was upon him; and with
his stripes we are healed.*

—Isaiah 53:4,5

NOT PERFECT, BUT NOT FORSAKEN

The simplest and most profound aspect of Christianity is found
in the death, burial, and resurrection of Jesus Christ. It was
upon the cross that He died as a sacrifice, or as Timothy says,
… a ransom for all… (1 Timothy 2:6 NKJV). All areas of human
existence were provided for by grace through faith in Jesus
Christ.

*Surely he hath borne our griefs, and carried our
sorrows: yet we did esteem him stricken, smitten
of God, and afflicted. But he was wounded for our
transgressions, he was bruised for our iniquities: the
chastisement of our peace was upon him; and with
his stripes we are healed.*

—Isaiah 53:4,5

The total man—spirit, soul, and body—was recovered by the
work of Jesus. Eternal salvation came by putting God's own life
inside of us by the Holy Ghost. The light of His Spirit flooded
into the darkness that dominated our spirits. Our minds were
given access to the very mind of God so that we can know His
will, His plans, and experience the very peace and joy of God.
Our worries, grief, and sorrows were replaced with His love,

faith, and power. Finally, our bodies were purchased by the blood of Jesus, and we were given access to His healing power. Then He gave us authority to go in this new power and show others how they too can get free and stay free.

God has not forsaken you. He never gives up on us. He loves everyone and wants to help us. He extends His love and help to those who have experienced the disillusionment of divorce and the chains of addictions. God's love is for the woman who had an abortion and feels dirty, used, and guilty. He is there for those who are in the grip of cynicism and have given up on the church. He is reaching out to those bound by religious ritual and legalistic performance.

Religion is not a bad word in itself. Religion is a system of practices based on one's beliefs in God. Man is innately religious. Most people have some kind of faith in God, but Satan takes that desire to experience God and perverts it into a form of godliness. He tricks man into believing that he can attain a relationship with God through his own human works. He recreates the image of God so that man sees God as one who does not allow for mistakes and punishes weakness and failure. Satan is very deceptive, blinding people's minds so that they have no understanding of the way God really feels about them. His most powerful tools are guilt and shame. "Shame would drive mankind in the wrong direction—away from the presence of Father. This is the destructive power of shame. Rather than draw us to the place of healing it drives us to run and hide from God and others. Unable to bear the guilt of our actions we hunt for places of seclusion that result in a numbing sense of loneliness."[1] Satan uses our experiences to convince us that life can never be lived at a higher level.

For years I preached and lived a distorted view of the gospel, thinking, *This is just how it is, hard and almost impossible.*

I knew that Jesus was the Son of God, but I could not seem to connect this truth with my actions. Temptation challenged my weaknesses as guilt nagged at my conscience. The result was an inward pressing against my insides, which produced a depressing, striving, rules-oriented, Christian lifestyle. I had created a dark recipe, mixing the spirit of religion with the glorious message of Jesus Christ. Religion had taught me that God does not love you until you get more holy and righteous, or until you achieve some type of status and recognition inside the church. I tried to define my life with my position and my works. Works and status are nice, but they have no power against the indulgence of the flesh, the world, and the devil.

> *These things indeed have an appearance of wisdom in self-imposed religion, false humility, and neglect of the body, but are of no value against the indulgence of the flesh.*
> —Colossians 2:23 NKJV

The problem with the voice of religion is that you can never do enough, even if you are doing good things. I spent ten years of ministry with these misconceptions. I loved God very much and was very active in church ministry. Inside I saw what God wanted me to do and be. God had placed destiny in my heart, but I was trying to fulfill that destiny through my own efforts, which only produced a field of frustration. Religious spirits love to see you working hard and feeling constant guilt about your inabilities to live up to God's righteous standards. Religious spirits love to remind you of your failures, because they don't want you to understand how easy it is to receive the freedom, power, joy, and victory of God's grace.

Many people, at one time or another, have sensed the desire to become a Christian. They tried and tried, but met only discouragement and failure. Many are outside of the church today, hurting and bitter because of the internal struggle that is defeating them. Many are disillusioned by their failed attempts at experiencing a personal relationship with God and the promised life of miracles and power that they have heard others talk about. They live in a spiritual dumpster, thinking their religious failures have destined them for an unknown eternity.

But the good news about the grace of Jesus Christ is that if you do not have any faith, God will give you some. Romans 12:3 says, *God has dealt to each one a measure of faith* (NKJV). Ephesians 2:8 says, *For by grace you have been saved through faith, and <u>that not of yourselves; it is the gift of God,</u> not of works, lest anyone should boast* (NKJV).

I have more good news for you! If you feel like you don't have any love, be encouraged, because God promised to give that love to you. *The love of God has been poured out in our hearts by the Holy Spirit who was given to us* (Romans 5:5 NKJV). What's the point? Regardless of what you think, what you feel, or what you have been told—God says He will never give up on you! It is

Regardless of what you think, what you feel, or what you have been told—God says He will never give up on you!

true that on your own you are not worthy. Isaiah 64:6 tells us that ...*all our righteousnesses are as filthy rags....* But by God's grace, you are made righteous. And your divine purpose, when realized, will ignite a joy and peace based on the secure reality that God is for you. If God were going to give up on you, He would have done it a long time ago—the first five, six, seven,

or eight times that you messed up. But, thank goodness, God never gives up on you.

You may be thinking that God only saves us when we are holy, but that is not true. God does not save us because we are holy, but because we have faith in Him and trust what He has done on our behalf. You might feel like giving up on yourself, but God will never give up on you. His saving hand will continually work to bring you to the place that He has prepared for you. Jesus made that promise, saying He was going to prepare a place for you. You may believe that it's too difficult and too much of a struggle. And it may be, but God will never give up on you! He will get you to the place that has been prepared for you.

GOD USES THE FOOLISH—
ARE YOU AVAILABLE?

> *But God has chosen the foolish things of the world to put to shame the wise, and God has chosen the weak things of the world to put to shame the things which are mighty.*
> —1 Corinthians 1:27 NKJV

God is looking for people who will humble themselves and allow the power of the Holy Spirit to lift them and empower them with a higher call. This is not just a "try to get by in life" call, but it's a call that is filled with an abundant reality of God's kingdom. God is not some mystical being hidden in a spiritual maze of religious ritual. He is God of the individual and God of the multitudes. He cares for the ninety and nine but is ready to go off looking for one lost sheep.

Most of the time, we try to formalize our relationship with Jesus Christ into a process, as though some kind of human formula will help us find our destiny. That is why we see the Christian life as such a struggle. It cannot be reduced to a religious recipe concocted in the mixing bowl of human effort. We must meet and know Jesus Christ on a personal basis and walk and talk with Him daily. The only place of true satisfaction is in the will of God and allowing Him to guide us. Sometimes this starts with making a decision to simply trust the way Jesus has prepared for those who will follow Him.

There are a lot of people who feel pretty foolish in their walk with God. They feel foolish and insecure about their ability to live up to their idea of God's standards. They feel foolish about their ability to live up to all the righteous requirements of the law, the struggles that come in the flesh, and the falls that we take in our journey when we walk with God. But God tells us in His Word that He takes the foolish things of the world and puts to shame the wise. How many of you have ever felt weak?

> *And the base things* [lowly or insignificant things]
> *of the world and the things which are despised God*
> *has chosen, and the things which are not, to bring*
> *to nothing the things that are, that no flesh should*
> *glory in His presence.*
> —1 Corinthians 1:28,29 NKJV

God takes the drug addict, the prostitute, the alcoholic, the murderer, anybody. He chooses those who will choose Him. God does not hold us back because of our backgrounds or our failures, regardless of what stiff, unforgiving religion might say. That would contradict the very theme of God's message to men. It is good news to know that God will never give up on you!

God's gospel call goes out to everybody. All He asks of us is to call on the name of the Lord, and seek Him with our whole heart. The Bible says, *that no flesh should glory in His presence.*

God says that our education, degrees, intellect, and opinions have no bearing on the Word and the will of God. They help in the secular world, but they do not have any bearing on the will and Word of God. *No flesh should glory in His presence.* This means that if you feel like you have to obtain a certain degree before God will help you or work with you, you are wrong. God will work with you right where you are if you are willing to work with Him.

THE POWER OF GOD'S GRACE

It is impossible to live an empowered Christian life unless we know the nature of God's grace. God's grace is powerful, and He is always willing to use that power for us when we need it. God reaches into our lives and lifts us up as we begin to surrender to Him. Grace is a power and a presence.

Grace makes its presence real in our lives by releasing God's power in us so that real change begins to take place, not some counterfeit forged by religious activity. The Holy Spirit begins to put a love for God and an understanding of spiritual things inside of us. Then we, by His help, begin praying these spiritual truths into existence. This is not something we can do through the exercise of our own power. That is what grace is all about.

As grace is released, God supernaturally begins to deposit and stir certain characteristics of himself inside of us, gradually creating an entire new way of thinking and responding. He fills us with *love, joy, peace, patience, kindness, goodness, faithfulness, gentleness, self-control*—the fruit of the Spirit (Galatians 5:22,23 NASB).

The kingdom of God is…righteousness, and peace, and joy in the Holy Ghost (Romans 14:17). When we allow His Spirit to lead and guide us, He automatically begins instilling His character into our being.

> *But of Him you are in Christ Jesus, who became for us wisdom from God—and righteousness and sanctification and redemption—that, as it is written, He who glories, let him glory in the LORD.*
> —1 Corinthians 1:30,31 NKJV

Christ becomes in us what we could not produce on our own. He becomes for us: wisdom from God, righteousness, and sanctification. That means you are set apart because He becomes that for you. You may be thinking, *Well, I just can't be holy enough.* That is right, and you do not have to be. The scripture says that He becomes sanctification for you. If you are in

Christ becomes in us what we could not produce on our own.

love with Him and walking towards Him, then you are walking away from the things that imprisoned you.

If you are troubled about the long-awaited perfection that seems to elude you, then let me remind you that all of God's promises hinge on you staying in the outburst of God's daily grace in your life. When we humble ourselves and focus on the wonders of God's kingdom through Christ Jesus, His Spirit invades our lives with wisdom, faith, and overcoming power. God will never give up on you!

We will not get to heaven and respond to God by saying, "I had the baptism in the Holy Ghost because I was pure and righteous and holy. I got here today because I attended church, said my prayers, and paid my tithe."

We will not get to heaven because of our exalted efforts. We will get there because the grace of God carried us all the way home. We know that if it was not for His grace, His mercy, and His loving-kindness, we would not be anywhere with Him today. It is He who called us, and He will perform it.

> *Therefore, having been justified by faith, we have peace with God through our Lord Jesus Christ, through whom also we have access by faith into this grace in which we stand, and rejoice in hope of the glory of God. And not only that, but we also glory in tribulations, knowing that tribulation produces perseverance [endurance]; and perseverance, character; and character, hope. Now hope does not disappoint, because the love of God has been poured out in our hearts by the Holy Spirit who was given to us.*
> —Romans 5:1-5 NKJV

We stand on the solid rock of the grace of God. We do not stand on our inability to keep things together in our lives—that is sinking sand. We will live in perpetual irritation if we seek to walk our Christian walk in our own natural abilities. We cannot do it, because God's thoughts are higher than our thoughts, and His ways are higher than our ways. He is not coming back for people just because they can shout the loudest, sing the best, or talk in tongues. He is coming back for people who have godly character.

He is looking for the fruit of the Spirit, not the fruit of our own ability. He produces His life within us as we submit to Him, call on His name, and say each day, "Oh, God, I am nothing without Your mercy and grace. Please do a work in my life."

It is then that God can use us. It is then that God will begin to develop that spiritual reality within our lives. Jesus made a provision for us when He returned to His Father. He gave the Holy Spirit to us, which is just like having Jesus with us all the time. He left the love of God with us, a love that encourages and empowers us to live for Him.

LOVE LIFTED ME

There is a lot of artificial love in the world today, and there is a deficiency of the love of God in the church. Everybody talks about love, but few people experience love because they are looking for love in all the wrong places.

Until we know the love of God, we will continue to endure rejection and experience loneliness. We allow ourselves to be offended and rejected by people, circumstances, places, and things because we do not understand the breadth and the width of God's love for us. God's love brings a power and poise to our lives regardless of the actions of others.

God's love brings a power and poise to our lives regardless of the actions of others.

How can you know God's love? By surrendering, yielding, and making your entire being available to Him. Grace is for the humble who are not afraid to recognize that they need a little help from heaven's hand.

> *For when we were still without strength, in due time Christ died for the ungodly, for scarcely for a righteous man will one die; yet perhaps for a good man*

would one even dare to die. But God demonstrates
His own love towards us, in that while we were still
sinners, Christ died for us.

—Romans 5:6-8 NKJV

Christ died for us. He did not wait until He had ten people gathered together who said, "Lord, if You die, we'll follow You." He initiated the action before men really understood how much they needed His help.

I would say that Jesus made the very first act of faith when He willingly died for people who didn't even know about Him yet. Not knowing if man would even accept His sacrifice, He paid the price to set men free.

If you feel like giving up because you don't feel like you ever please God, now is the time to let go and trust Him. All you have to do is humble yourself and trust the plan that He designed for your life. His original plan was for Jesus to exit through Heaven's gates and descend into the dark world of your despair with a message of the Father's love and an action to demonstrate that love.

Most of us will not give love unless someone loves us first and we know that they are going to treat us just right. We are not willing to risk rejection. But Jesus risked the rejection of man and offered His uncompromising love.

Jesus gives His love to you anyway. He just asks that you reach out towards Him as a sign of your desire to love Him. And when you do, He will work with you. He knows that you are not perfect and never will be perfect through your own efforts, but He is calling you, and He wants to work with you today.

Keep a humble heart towards the Lord, and no matter how many times life knocks you down, you can know that God is working in the background. He sees, He knows, and He does care!

A man in the Bible named Gideon felt like he could not be used of God because of his own insecurity. You may be thinking, *But Gideon was a man who served God.* No. Gideon came from a family that talked about Jehovah, and they were part of the tribes of Israel, but his family actually lived a life of compromise and idolatry. They mixed the faith of their forefathers with the worship of Baal, and they made wooden images that were worshiped also.

Gideon was raised in the midst of religious compromise and infidelity. The days in which he lived were similar to our times today. Many people say they are Christians, but they are not committed to seeing the kingdom of God grow, which is His purpose. The majority of people are more wrapped up in worshiping self, fishing, hunting, cars, clothes, jewelry, television, and anything else that takes priority over their relationship with God. It is not wrong to participate in these things, but if your exposure to the mixture of these things causes them to become priorities in your life, then you can relate to Gideon. Such mixed priorities always blind your spiritual and moral eyesight, and limit your ability to see God working in the shadows of your life.

Notice that the scripture says Gideon was bitter towards God. He even questioned where God was and where the miracles were that his father had once seen. He questioned where God was when he was in need of Him.

Have you ever felt that way towards God? This is where most people live, wondering where the miracle-working power of God is in their lives. They walk around without faith— unhappy, depressed, and bitter.

The God of grace is a God of restoration and hope. He has a plan, and His plan comes with power, strength, and love that

reaches out to us and asks for our willingness to receive His power through Jesus Christ. God never gives up on us!

The God of grace is a God of restoration and hope.

Because Christ's sacrifice of love extended to all mankind through the giving of His life, God worked a plan that linked a spiritual world to a human, fleshly, mentally based world of humanity. Through this process of redemption, mankind is allowed access to heaven's resources and a whole new life of reality through God's Holy Spirit.

When you have a meeting with God, just you and Him, it will change your life forever. Peace, joy, and righteousness can be a daily benefit in your life. God is no respecter of persons. He has no personal favorites. God loves you, and He wants your life to be full of abundant living. God never gets tired of forgiving and helping. Do you know why? **Because God will never give up on you!**

GOD HAS A PLAN FOR YOUR LIFE!

> *Then the children of Israel did evil in the sight of the LORD. So the LORD delivered them into the hand of Midian for seven years, and the hand of Midian prevailed against Israel. Because of the Midianites, the children of Israel made for themselves the dens, the caves, and strongholds which are in the mountains. So it was, whenever Israel had sown, the Midianites would come up; also the Amalekites and the people of the East would come up against them.*

Then they would encamp against them and destroy the produce of the earth as far as Gaza, and leave no sustenance for Israel, neither sheep nor ox nor donkey. For they would come up with their livestock and their tents, coming in as numerous as locusts; both they and their camels were without number; and they would enter the land to destroy it. So, Israel was greatly impoverished because of the Midianites, and the children of Israel cried out to the Lord. And it came to pass, when the children of Israel cried out unto the Lord because of the Midianites, that the Lord sent a prophet to the children of Israel, who said to them, "Thus says the Lord God of Israel: 'I brought you up from Egypt and brought you out of the house of bondage; and I delivered you out of the hand of the Egyptians and out of the hand of all who oppressed you, and drove them out before you and gave you their land, also I said to you, "I am the Lord your God; do not fear the gods of the Amorites, in whose land you dwell, But you have not obeyed My voice.""

—Judges 6:1-10 NKJV

God is reality! Maybe you are not sure what God wants to do for you, or sometimes you might feel stuck, trapped in your circumstances. God has been in the miracle business for a long time, and He is still open 24 hours a day. So as we review Gideon's circumstances, I want you to see what kind of man God was working with. It makes no difference to God whether you are

God has been in the miracle business for a long time, and He is still open 24 hours a day.

rich or poor, black or white, male or female. God loves you, and He will never give up on you. There is a way out! There is light at the end of the tunnel! Let's take a walk through Gideon's world and see how to live a more powerful, joyous, and prosperous life.

Midian or *Midianite* means "strife." *Amalekite* means "sorrowful, weary from worry, iniquity, wickedness, miserable, a weathering of body or mind." How many people do you know who are not very old in age, yet they are already weathered by the worries of life? Their minds are fried from the constant struggles of facing life without peace in their soul or real joy inside.

The first thing we notice about the children of Israel is the oppression. They were consigned to living in caves.

Many of you are living in caves of fear, depression, poverty, and divorce. These and many other debilitating conditions drive people into hiding. Living in these oppressed conditions often leads to seeking happiness through drugs, alcohol, and illicit sex. These people, like Gideon, are seeking all kinds of other things—things that God never intended to be a source of peace.

The second problem Israel faced was that every time they planted seeds, the Midianites and Amalekites would come to destroy and steal from them. How many of you feel like this every time you think you are doing right? Just when you think you are making progress, all of a sudden the devil comes in and wipes you out. It seems like every time you get something going, there the devil is again to pluck up those seeds. It is almost as if he goes behind you with a little shovel, digging them up as soon as you plant them. The Bible says that whenever Israel sowed, the enemy came in. And that's what he does to us today, but this is not the time to give up. If you are doing the best you can to surrender to Jesus Christ, then hold on tight. Your day is coming. Keep pressing on even though life keeps throwing you curves. Perhaps you lost a job, a special relationship ended, or a friend betrayed you. How you react to these curve balls makes all the difference. If you get angry and give up, then you will miss your date with opportunity. When your life is skidding out of control, you have to turn into the skid. Hang in there, for he who endures to the end will be saved.

Thirdly, the enemies of Israel were looking down their throats. Staring them down, they were ready to steal the blessings of Israel. So it is in your life. Jesus said, *"The thief comes only to steal, and kill, and destroy..."* (John 10:10 NASB). The enemy comes to take the blessings—the prosperity, the calling, and the joy—that God has for you. Don't fall prey to his evil plan. Do not let him steal what God has given to you. He can't take your blessings unless you let him. The scripture says, *Resist the devil and he will flee from you* (James 4:7 NASB). You have the authority to speak to the devil and tell him to stop it. Confront him with the authority of heaven in your heart and command him to go!

When the evil plan of the Midianites and Amalekites was accomplished, the Israelites were left with no *sustenance*— no food, supplies, or livelihood. The enemy left nothing for them to eat. This seems oppressive, but just wait until Gideon shows up on the scene. A day of reckoning was coming for the enemies of God.

"Our daily routines may make us feel worthless, and our families may at times make us feel unloved, but as we spend time in the presence of God, we are reminded that we are His precious children, purchased with a great price, beloved, and valued."[2]

RESPONDING TO YOUR CIRCUMSTANCES

The protagonist, Gideon, enters this tragic scene in Judges 6:11. The first thing you must remember when confronting conflicting circumstances is that God is still with you. The Lord strong and mighty is with you. Even if you do not feel Him, He is watching you. He knows you by name. He has a plan for your life, a plan to give you hope and a future. He cares about your marriage, your job, and your entire life. He will show you the way out if you are willing to follow His lead. It is not a temporary solution, but an eternal resolution that brings victory to your life.

His way, His plans, and His leading will bring you out of uncertainty and into a life of freedom. It is not the absence of our problems that gives us peace; it is God's presence *in* the problem that will bring peace. In Judges 6:12, the angel said, *The LORD is with you* (NASB). You must remember: *If God be for us, who can be against us?* (Romans 8:31). With God on your side, a majority has been created. Your enemies are now outnumbered no matter what the odds.

The second thing you must remember is how God sees you. It is important to know that God's view of your life is much different from yours. He is not disappointed with your fear, nor is He disillusioned with your failure. You are important to Him. Jesus is the conduit of God's love that is flowing to you. God sees you as someone who qualifies for all the benefits of the kingdom of God. You are now of God's royal family.

God sees you as someone who qualifies for all the benefits of the kingdom of God.

So regardless of how you feel, God sees you as a person who deserves all of heaven's resources. Do not waste your time feeling worthless. You are accepted, so just accept God's decision on your life. Robert Capon put it well when he said, "God won't stop telling us how good we are, but we won't shut up long enough to trust His judgment."³

No problem is too large for God's intervention; no person is too small for God's attention. God sent an angel to tell Gideon that he was a mighty man of valor. It was hard for Gideon to see himself as some spiritual giant. When the angel of God came to Gideon, he was oppressed, poor, bitter, and he was the youngest in his family.

Valor means "a force, an army, war worthy; a company of great forces; ability, virtue, strength, power, riches, and substance." The main four words mean "strength, army, wealth, and produce"— the very things that Gideon was not and did not have. God said, "You are, and you have." It reminds me of another scripture in the book of Joel, *Let the weak say, I am strong* (3:10). God calls those things that are not as though they are.

God sees you through the eyes of Jesus Christ. He sees you through the blood of Jesus Christ. You are the apple of His eye. God chooses to see you this way. As long as He sees you this way, then you are on His side, and He is on your side. You have access to Him, His weapons, and His abilities, and no devil in hell can overcome you! Remember this when you feel like God is not there. **Remember how God sees you.**

> *Gideon said to Him, "Oh my lord, if the LORD is with us, why then has all this happened to us? And where are all His miracles which our fathers told us about, saying, 'Did not the LORD bring us up from Egypt?' But now the LORD has forsaken us and delivered us into the hands of the Midianites."*
> —Judges 6:13 NKJV

I can just hear Gideon now. It reminds me of some of you when your pastor tries to give you an encouraging word. You respond with, "Where is God now, and how come I've been in this place for so long?" Or, "God must not care about me, because He sure doesn't seem to be around when I need Him."

Gideon had never seen the miracles. He had only heard about them, and he was questioning if they were really for his day. Sound familiar?

In verse 14, notice that the angel of the Lord ignored Gideon's whining and complaining. He was probably just waiting for Gideon to finish griping so he could receive the answer. *Then the LORD turned to [Gideon] and said, "Go in this might of yours, and you shall save Israel from the hand of the Midianites. Have I not sent you?"* (Judges 6:14 NKJV).

The third thing you have to remember when you think God has forsaken you is to turn your anger into action. Turn your anger away from God and yourself and face your enemy. Take the frustration, hurt, anger, and loneliness, or whatever negative factors and emotions that may be at work against you, and move in another direction. It is painful to confront our own failures with honesty and objectivity, yet that is the only path to correcting attitudes and actions that may have contributed to the behavior.

Transform those negative emotions of failure and discouragement into faith and trust in the Word of the Lord.

If you know who God is and how He sees you, and you understand that He is not mad at you and has not given up on you, then get up and get ready for something wonderful to happen to you. Transform those negative emotions of failure and discouragement into faith and trust in the Word of the Lord.

God knows the struggles and questions that are in our hearts. That's why the angel of the Lord didn't say to Gideon, "Ah ha, you just blew it! How dare you question the miracles of

God?" If our struggles and questions could blow our relationship with God, then we would all be in trouble. But the angel just ignored the fit Gideon was throwing, and reminded him that God said, *"Go in this might of yours."* He was trying to get Gideon to take that zeal and energy and all that was inside of him and use it against the enemy. ***The Lord is with you! Go!***

When you are feeling angry and bitter at God, feeling like He must have forsaken you, take those troublesome feelings to the Lord. Get on your knees and pray, and hold on until heaven comes down. If God is God—and He is—then He will come through for you! You better believe that when you do that, God has got a miracle waiting for you!

Gideon said, *"Oh my Lord, how can I save Israel? Indeed my clan is the weakest in Manasseh, and I am the least in my father's house." And the* LORD *said to him, "Surely I will be with you, and you shall defeat the Midianites as one man"* (Judges 6:15,16 NKJV).

The word *least* here means "little, few, young in age and moral value." God doesn't always call you when you feel strong. He enjoys using those who are weak and less likely to succeed. Most of the time, He calls you to a new place in Him when you are not doing very well.

Gideon was saying, "How can I do this God?" That is what most of us say when we are faced with a challenge. The Word comes to us, and we walk out thinking and saying to ourselves, "This will never work. I don't know how God could do this for me. That message must have been for somebody else. I guess I'll never be free, because it's been too long now."

No! Do not say that. God can do whatever He wants. Matthew 19:26 says, *"…with God* all *things are possible."* Gideon said, "Me and my family are poor." The word *poor* means "impoverished or oppressed." Gideon was saying, "Lord, You're telling me to go deliver a nation, but I feel dried up, empty, oppressed, feeble, and weak. I feel like a failure, lowly and not equal to anybody else. Someone else must be better for the job." These words didn't exactly set the stage for success.

Author Warren Bennis interviewed seventy very successful business executives, and not one referred to his past mistakes as failures. They chose terms like "learning experiences, detours, or opportunities for growth."[4] There is a good lesson here. You can't allow your negative assessment of your circumstances to keep you from fulfilling God's plan for your life.

Never accept your present, temporary situations as your future or permanent situations.

If you sit back and allow life to keep pushing you around, you will always remain a victim. Circumstances are automatically waiting on you to tell them what to do and how to change. You can't just wait on an opportunity. Never accept your present, temporary situations as your future or permanent situations. In times of adversity, you don't have an obstacle to deal with; you have a choice to make. Most of the time, the first action is to change your attitude. It has been said that attitude is altitude. Well, then let go of the weights of criticism, hurt, anger, and remorse. Let this be a new day. Begin changing the way you speak. Talk faith, hope, and love, which is God's language. God does not take the back roads, so take the highways of God and soar in altitude by changing your attitude. Choose God's reaction and do not judge your action by circumstances.

God wants you to see what He is. Gideon told the Lord what little he had to work with. No money, no political pull, no contacts. How was he going to get people to follow him in order to deliver a nation?

"Title, position and power are not enough to make a leader. Strength of character and a person's inner qualities are what determines genuine leadership."[5]

You do not have to be "somebody" in this world for God to use you. You already are "somebody" with God! The declaration of the unfailing love of God puts circumstances in proper perspective.

> *So Gideon went in and prepared a young goat, and unleavened bread from an ephah of flour. The meat he put in a basket, and he put the broth in a pot; and he brought them out to Him under the terebinth tree and presented them. The Angel of God said to him, "Take the meat and the unleavened bread and lay them on this rock, and pour out the broth." And he did so.*
> —Judges 6:19,20 NKJV

Remember, you have to make yourself available. The New Testament says, *...present your bodies a living sacrifice, holy, acceptable to God, which is your reasonable service* (Romans 12:1 NKJV). How did Gideon make himself available? The angel instructed Gideon to take the meat and bread and *"lay them on this rock."* Who is the Rock? Jesus Christ. Make yourself a sacrifice and lay it on Christ Jesus, on His Word, and leave it there. Grace (God's willingness to use His power and ability on your behalf) is a powerful force. It has already been sent from heaven to help you in your time of need. Yield, surrender, and let grace work in you. If you fall down, get back up. Keep surrendering, and let God refresh and empower you; then keep going. No matter how many times you have been knocked down, get back up. The true test of one's spiritual maturity is not how often he falls, but how quickly he gets back up. Keep asking God to help you. He will because He said He would. Do not lose heart! Be encouraged and keep yourself available. Tell God over and

The true test of one's spiritual maturity is not how often he falls, but how quickly he gets back up.

over, "I love You, and I will serve You. Here I am, God, and I thank You for continuing to believe in me." Tell Him that every day. Every time things seem hard, tell Him again.

The angel then instructed Gideon to *"pour out the broth."* That means to "let it all go." Pour it all out on the altar—the disappointment, anger, rejection, and hurt—and let it all go.

When you feel that God has given up on you, remember that *...he is able to keep that* which [you have] *committed unto Him...* (2 Timothy 1:12). If He promised it, He will perform it. *He who calls you is faithful, who also will do it* (1 Thessalonians 5:24 NKJV). *He who has begun a good work in you will complete it...* (Philippians 1:6).

> *Then the Angel of the LORD put out the end of his staff that was in His hand, and touched the meat and the unleavened bread; and fire rose out the rock and consumed the meat and the unleavened bread. And the Angel of the Lord departed out of his sight. Now Gideon perceived that He was the Angel of the Lord. So Gideon said, "Alas, Oh Lord GOD! For I have seen the Angel of the LORD face to face."*
> —Judges 6:21,22 NKJV

When you commit your life to God and come to the point that you give everything to Him, holding nothing back, then

He will touch you, fire you up, and consume that thing that you laid on the Rock before Him. If you will continually present yourself, your future, and your entire life to Him, He will be faithful and happy to continue leading you into all the blessings He has for you. God is never the problem. He never leaves us. We are the ones who bail out on Him. We have a tendency to get distracted by our own pursuits. But as soon as we surrender to Him, He will continue to keep that which has been committed unto Him.

PEACE, PEACE, WONDERFUL PEACE

> *Then the LORD said to him "Peace be with you; do not fear, you shall not die." So Gideon built an altar there to the LORD, and called it The-LORD-Is-Peace.*
> —Judges 6:23,24 NKJV

If you truly trust in God, you will have peace, even when your surroundings are in turmoil; even when things are not exactly as you had hoped they would be. You can have peace when you have to believe God for your rent money or when your body is sick and falling apart. Peace can be yours even when you feel addicted and degraded by the garbage that was in your life before you became a Christian. Before God can move in your life, you must be at peace, knowing that everything is in His hands.

A lot of the struggles we have in our search for peace are the result of refusing to trust God. There are a lot of things that we cannot resolve, but they will never be resolved until we turn them over to God so that He can work them out.

Gideon built an altar, and he worshiped and praised God. He praised Him when he was still in the middle of his troubles. He was not free of his troubles yet. He did not have the rent money. He did not have his needs met. The enemy was still staring him down. He didn't even have what God had promised him yet. He was still oppressed, still in bondage, but something came into his spirit, and he began to trust in God. Because of that trust, he had peace.

Peace is an excellent monitor to understanding the will of God. After you learn to receive God's grace, you start to sense His love and acceptance, and peace is the result. Do not fear or hesitate. Hold on to His promises. When you praise God for who He is, what He did, and what He's going to do, then peace will flow into your life like a river. This is the power of grace.

Grace IN ACTION

"For this very purpose I have raised you up, that I may show My power in you, and that My name may be declared in all the earth."
—Romans 9:17 NKJV

God has raised you up and empowered you to share His name in the earth.

His grace—His willingness to use His power and ability on your behalf—is a powerful force. And He has given that grace to you to pass on to others. What a privilege and responsibility!

The devil is busy in today's world, doing all he can to blind the eyes of as many people as possible. But you have the power to counter that attack with the truth and love of God. Are you ready to declare His name through the power He has vested in you? It is an act of love and obedience that will be well worth the effort.

Chapter Five

Grace — Just Seems Too Good To Be True

Jesus went unto the mount of Olives. And early in the morning he came again into the temple, and all the people came unto him; and he sat down, and taught them. And the scribes and Pharisees brought unto him a woman taken in adultery; and when they had set her in the midst, they say unto him, Master, this woman was taken in adultery, in the very act. Now Moses in the law commanded us, that such should be stoned: but what sayest thou? This they said, tempting him, that they might have to accuse him. But Jesus stooped down, and with his finger wrote on the ground, as though he heard them not. So when they continued asking him, he lifted up himself, and said unto them, He that is without sin among you, let him first cast a stone at her. And again he stooped down, and wrote on the ground. And they which heard it, being convicted by their own conscience, went out one by one, beginning at the eldest, even unto the last: and Jesus was left alone, and the woman standing in the midst. When Jesus had lifted up himself, and saw none but the woman, he said unto her, Woman, where are those thine accusers? hath no man condemned thee? She said, No man, Lord. And Jesus said unto her, Neither do I condemn thee: go, and sin no more.

—John 8:1-11

The Mount of Olives is located east of Jerusalem on a mountain ridge above the city, and is mentioned a couple of times in the Old Testament. The first mention is when King David was fleeing Jerusalem during the time of Absalom's rebellion in 2 Samuel 15:30. *And David went up by the ascent of mount Olivet, and wept as he went up, and had his head covered, and he went barefoot: and all the people that was with him covered every man his head, and they went up, weeping as they went up.*

The second time it is mentioned is in Zechariah 14:3,4, in reference to the time when God will establish His reign over all the nations. *Then shall the LORD go forth, and fight against those nations, as when he fought in the day of battle. And his feet shall stand in that day upon the mount of Olives, which is before Jerusalem on the east, and the mount of Olives shall cleave in the midst thereof toward the east and toward the west, and there shall be a very great valley; and half of the mountain shall remove toward the north, and half of it toward the south.*

Mount Olives, as it was often called, was a place of religion, and it was very important to the Jewish people. It was believed that here God would resurrect the dead.

"During the time of the first and second Temples, Mount Olives was the place where the high priest used to slaughter and burn the 'Red Cow', who's ashes purify the impure."[1]

Jesus was attracted to this solemn place and would often retreat to the Mount in order to teach His disciples or to find a place of rest from His ministry. On this occasion, Jesus went up the Mount of Olives, probably for a time of rest. It was often in these private moments that Jesus would get His instructions from the Father. Early the next morning, He descended and came to the temple. As usual, when Jesus arrived at any public place, people began to gather around Him. With every eye gazing on Him, Jesus began to teach them. As one of His disciples wrote, Jesus taught the people as one who had authority. There was a power and an

Jesus taught the people as one who had authority.

attraction in the words of Jesus, and every time He opened His mouth men were stunned and overwhelmed by the weight of His words on the human soul.

JESUS AND THE SINFUL WOMAN

On one occasion as Jesus was teaching, there was a disturbance at the back of the crowd that surrounded Jesus. Jesus looked towards the back as the scribes and Pharisees were shoving men and women aside in their determined attempt to reach the Master. Caught in their clutches was a woman who had been discovered in the act of adultery. One wonders if this woman had a shady reputation and the religious leaders had designed a trap for her. They had caught her in the very act. How did that happen? However it happened, these religious men had found the woman engaged in breaking the law.

Dragging the woman behind them, these religious men finally reached the front. Viciously, they threw the woman down at Jesus' feet. They thrust their pointed fingers at her with words of condemnation spurting from their lips. They began to describe to Jesus how they had caught this woman in an adulterous act.

The Pharisees went on to *explain* to Jesus what the law had to say concerning her situation—*she must be stoned to death.* In disgust, they turned their eyes from the woman and looked at Jesus, and in chorus, they questioned Him. *What do you say about this?*

Now, here is something you should never forget. When religious men ask a question, it is usually a trap. They aren't interested in hearing your pearls of wisdom. They are more interested in seeing if you are standing within the circle of their orthodoxy.

In this instance, the Pharisees were trying to catch Jesus in a heretical statement so they could stone Him alongside of the sinful woman. They were tempting Him that they might find something with which to accuse Him. What would you do in this situation? On one hand, the law demanded that she be stoned. Yet on the other hand, Jesus had been preaching the message of grace and love. If He agreed with them, it would confirm their judgmental attitudes. If He disagreed, they would condemn Him. Would He submit to what the law demanded or what His heart desired for this imprisoned woman?

Jesus always had the right words for situations like this. Noting their devious attempts to trap Him, Jesus countered their trap with a trap of His own. Silently, Jesus knelt down and began to move His finger through the dusty ground. What was He writing? We don't know exactly what He wrote on the ground, but whatever it was, it stopped the Pharisees dead cold. Some suggest that He might have written a description of their own sins. We don't know, but whatever it was, it was effective. The religious leaders inched closer so they could read His words. Their mouths were shut by the words written in the sandy soil. Lifting His eyes up to them, Jesus softly said, "He that is without sin among you, let him cast the first stone at her." Then He stooped down and wrote on the ground again. Whatever He wrote, conviction rained down on them, and starting with the eldest to the youngest, they dropped their proud heads and walked away.

Jesus then turned His attention to the woman who was standing there shocked at what she has just witnessed. She knew what she could expect at the hands of the Pharisees, but she didn't know what to expect from this man whose eyes were staring straight into her heart. After what seemed like an eternity, Jesus finally spoke, "Woman where are your accusers? Has no man condemned you?" Looking at Him she said, "No man, Lord." Bringing this scene to an end, Jesus tells her, "Neither do I condemn thee; go and sin no more."

JESUS IS THE REASON WHY YOU SHOULD NOT GIVE UP!

Jesus Christ was the bridge in keeping this woman from being stoned. He is also your bridge to keep you from giving up because of your failure and the resulting shame. A bad day or a bad month is no reason to turn your back on the only person who can rescue you from your painful past and calamitous circumstances. Christ is the reason why you can still go on.

We must not overlook the fact that this woman was *guilty*. She was guilty as charged and had no reason to be released!

The law was clear: she deserved death. But Jesus came to introduce a new law—the law of grace. In this story, we see the motion of grace as it extends its hand to those who have been knocked down by the reality of their situations. This is the basis of everything that Christ did on Calvary. You should be guilty, but because of faith in Christ, you're released from the tragedy of your trespasses.

Some might ask, "Is grace a reason why we should go on sinning?" No! Paul answered that in his letter to the Romans. The goodness of God leads you to a place of repentance. It empowers you to turn your back on your past.

When the religious cops busted you for violation of the law and you were brought into God's courtroom, He passed judgment in your favor.

Jesus made the first move so that you can take the second in response to His loving hand. He has covered your shame so that you can turn towards Him. When the religious cops busted you for violation of the law and you were brought into God's courtroom, He passed judgment in your favor. His favor silences the judgment of others and opens up the door for you to walk away from your sin.

We're talking about a gift! That's grace—it is favor that you do not deserve. In the courtroom of religious law, you have no defense. Nothing you have done or can do deserves this gift. It is not "all about you." It is "all about Him."

IT SEEMS TOO GOOD TO BE TRUE

We live in a world where rewards come from hard work or service. You work forty hours a week, and then you receive a check. You go to a restaurant and order a meal, and then you have to pay for it. Your paycheck is not free, and neither is that meal. Somebody has to work and somebody has to pay. Whenever we get something that we didn't work or pay for, then it seems too good to be true. That's just how it works in our culture. But in the culture of Christ, we get something for nothing. That is the power of grace.

The gifts of God do not come to you because you deserve them or are better than someone else. You had nothing to do with the gift. God's gifts are based on His character, not yours. He chooses to put that call and that destiny on your life because He cares for you.

How do you respond when you get something that is too good to be true? You must walk in a way that is worthy of the gift. Your life should reflect your appreciation of the gift. Your thankfulness should be expressed in the way that you live your life, honoring the one who has blessed you so richly.

Jesus bypasses the system in order to get the gift to you. We are not used to such gracious and gratuitous actions from others. Surely there must be something that we have to do. We have sinned, and we must perform some kind of penance. No. Grace is a gift. Laying down our pride, we must simply accept the gift for what it is—a free expression of our Father's love for us.

Laying down our pride, we must simply accept the gift for what it is—a free expression of our Father's love for us.

YOU ARE ACCEPTED IN THE BELOVED

If God looks at you and says you are blessed, healed, whole, and righteous, then merely accept the gift! In the Old Testament, when people brought their sacrifices to the priest, the priest would inspect the sacrifices, not the people. God looks at the sacrifice of His Son, not you. If the sacrifice is acceptable, then you are accepted. This is what Paul said in Ephesians 1:6, *To the praise of the glory of his grace, wherein he hath made us accepted in the beloved.* This is the glory of His grace—you are accepted. The German theologian, Paul Tillich described that glorious grace with these compelling words:

"Grace strikes us when we are in great pain and restlessness. It strikes us when we walk through the dark valley of a meaningless and empty life. It strikes us when, year after year, the longed-for perfection does not appear, when the old compulsions reign within us as they have for decades, when despair destroys all joy and courage. Sometimes at that moment a wave of light breaks into our darkness, and it is as though a great voice were saying: 'You are accepted. You are accepted, accepted by that which is greater than you...'"[2]

If the Lamb is accepted, then so are you. He is the spotless Lamb of God—the acceptable sacrifice. You are accepted in Him. Because He chose to step up in front of you and take the punishment for your sins, you have been set free.

Adam passed on the virus of sin to the whole human race. We were all born with the disadvantage of a sinful nature. Trapped in the cell of sin, Jesus came to our rescue. He stepped up and paid the price to set us free. For the guardians of jurisprudence, this is not acceptable, but in the court of Christ, their judgment is cancelled out. Again, I can hear you saying that it seems too good to be true. I agree with you. It is too good to be true, but ***it is true.***

What about keeping the commandments? Jesus reduced the 653 commandments of the Old Testament to 2 commandments. Jesus said to love God and love others. Grace reverses the negative trends in your life so that you are now able to fulfill the law—loving God and loving others (including yourself).

AGREE WITH GOD'S JUDGMENT ABOUT YOU

God sees us through the eyes of Christ and calls us holy. We cannot see what He sees, but we must accept what He sees. Don't be deceived by what you see. Learn to accept what He sees in you because of Christ. What you speak over your life is very important. You must be willing to call into existence those things that are not as though they are. Christ has become sanctification for you. You must agree with His view of who you are. When you do, a doorway of blessing will be opened to you.

All you have to do is yield to what Christ did for you in order to receive wisdom, peace, joy, and healing—then you can be what God has called you to be. He has given you access to the storehouse of heaven through the shed blood of Jesus Christ. He ripped down the curtain and said, "Come in here." Somebody else is pointing at you telling you that you don't deserve this favor. All the religious people are telling the Judge, "You don't know where they've been, and You don't know what they've been up to. This man was *caught in the act!"*

Jesus stopped all the condemnation and accusations against you. Jesus cancelled out the condemnation of others over your life. And the story is over! It's done! *The wisdom which none of the rulers of this age has understood; for if they had understood it, they would not have crucified the Lord of glory...* (1 Corinthians 2:8 NASB). If only they had understood, but they did not. They were locked in their own religious paradigms, and could

Religion is complicated, but the good news of Jesus Christ is very simple.

not escape so as to see the goodness of God that extended even to them. Religion is complicated, but the good news of Jesus Christ is very simple.

Now you must stop denying what He has done by focusing on all the negativity of your life. Simply acknowledge that what He has done has brought great benefits to your life. Learn to see through the eyes of Jesus. You must move from *sin consciousnesses* to *God consciousnesses*.

THE LAW AND THE PROPHETS
AGREE WITH JESUS

Paul told the Galatians that the law was to be our schoolmaster. The law is for the lawless. If you are under grace, you're going to pursue what's right anyway! God called priests and prophets to speak to the people according to the law. The law brought an understanding of sin.

But now the righteousness of God without the law is manifested, being witnessed by the law and the prophets; even the righteousness of God which is by faith of Jesus Christ unto all and upon all them that believe: for there is no difference (Romans 3:21,22). Unto whom? All! And upon all who believe, for there is no difference.

There is one key that unlocks this reality of righteousness—it is for all who believe. Faith is the key to heaven's realities. It is as simple as saying, "I understand the grace of God. I need it, I believe it, and by faith, I accept it and apply it to my life. I thank God that He's working with me while I'm working this out. Because of His blood, I am given a ticket to pass into the realm of grace's realities!"

That is why the goodness of God will lead you to repentance if you really understand His goodness! Romans 3:23 says, *For all have sinned, and come short of the glory of God.* According to the law, everyone is guilty in some way! But the problem of guilt is solved in verse 24, *...being justified freely by his grace through the redemption that is in Christ Jesus.* How are we justified?

How does God look upon us just as if we had never sinned? It is through the eyes of grace. You are made right through the redemption that is in Christ Jesus. You are justified or made right by God, not by any efforts of your own, but by what Jesus Christ did on Calvary. The law and the prophets are forced to accept this work of God on your behalf.

JESUS IS THE ANSWER TO YOUR SIN PROBLEM

Whom God hath set forth to be a propitiation through faith in his blood, to declare his righteousness for the remission of sins that are past, through the forbearance of God (Romans 3:25). God tarried through the process of resolving man's predicament until the law could be fulfilled in Christ. *For when we were yet without strength, in due time Christ died for the ungodly* (Romans 5:6). At just the right time, Christ came into the world. In Christ, God was manifest in the flesh. He was born sinless, of the virgin Mary, and made like unto us. He paid this price for us. God waited throughout the years for just the right moment in time. He tarried through the process of time in order to remedy Adam's sin and bring man home through Christ.

Paul is on a roll now. Revelation is flowing. In Romans 3:26, he tells us that God's actions were *to demonstrate at the present time His righteousness: that He might be just and the justifier of the one who has faith in Jesus* (NKJV). God played by the rules He had set up in order to free men from their sins and burdens, and He did it through

Jesus was God's answer to man's sin problem.

Jesus. Jesus was God's answer to man's sin problem. You have a problem with sin? Jesus is the answer to that problem.

After peeking into the purposes of God in Christ, Paul now turns his face towards man. In Romans 3:27, Paul presents this question to all of us: *Where is boasting then?* You want to talk about how good you are? By what law do your good works resolve your problem with sin? There is no law that says your good works can set you free from sin. It is only ...*by the law of faith* (NKJV).

You cannot be good enough to get forgiveness for your sins. You can't be holy enough to receive it. All that religious effort is in vain. Now, that is bad news for those who have been working for years and years to achieve acceptance through works. Forgiveness for sin only comes by faith in God's grace and in His finished work. Christ says, "I justify you, make you right, and I call you righteous in my sight."

Yes, it sounds too good to be true. But this is the good news of the gospel of Jesus Christ! I've actually had people say to me, "If you preach the message of grace, then what incentive will people have to serve God?" My reply is, "They serve God out of love and not out of duty." What better incentive is there?

Paul goes on to say that man is justified without the deeds of the law. This does not compute for the modern man who thinks that he must work for what he needs. But Paul is radically clear in saying that God's way is through the work of Christ, not through the work of man.

Skipping over to Romans 4:5, Paul announces, *But to him that worketh not, but **believeth** on Him that justifieth the*

Favor comes to those who, by faith, accept the gift.

ungodly, his faith is counted for righteousness. Paul says the only work you can do is to believe. The man who gets God's favor of grace is not the man who does works. His works gets him nothing. Favor comes to those who, by faith, accept the gift.

In verse 6, Paul goes on to say that even David talked about the man in whom God imputed righteousness without works.

David said in Psalm 32:1, *Blessed is he whose transgression is forgiven, whose sin is covered.* Paul concludes, *Blessed is the man to whom the Lord will not impute sin* (Romans 4:8). *Impute* means "paid to the account of another, or to pass over another who is guilty." Christ stepped up and covered us so that the enemy and the accuser could pass over us when he's looking to condemn us. Christ steps in front of us and says, "Where are your accusers?"

THE PROMISES OF ABRAHAM

Paul moves from David to Abraham in Romans 4:9, *Cometh this blessedness then upon the circumcision only, or upon the uncircumcision also? for we say that faith was reckoned to Abraham for righteousness.* Favor and blessings—it just keeps getting better. The same help, wealth, supernatural power, and promises that God gave to Abraham come to all, whether circumcised or not. Now, for the Jew, circumcision was a pretty important thing. It made them special. But Paul says the blessings of Abraham come to all, whether Jew or Greek. The same benefits and blessings that were given to Abraham are given to all.

Paul is working on some inductive reasoning here, guided by the Spirit. In verse 14, he reasons, *For if they which are of the law be heirs, faith is made void, and the promise made of none effect.* If those who are living by the law get the blessings, then this nullifies the power of faith. He is saying that if you try to get the promises by trying to act right, then you are making a huge mistake. This is good news to all those people who are so desperate for God. Even if you just can't keep the rules and regulations, that's all right, because He

If you feel like you just can't do it, He's got you covered—He did it for you.

is able. Even if you feel like you just can't do it, He's got you covered—He did it for you.

In Romans 4:16, Paul continues with this thought, *Therefore it is of faith, that it might be by grace....* Now we have reached the critical moment in Paul's defense of grace. Completing the verse, he says, *to the end the promise might be sure to all the seed; not to that only which is of the law, but to that also which is of the faith of Abraham; who is the father of us all.*

This is great news. The promise is to all who believe. It is for the Jew, and it is for you. To those who have exhausted their religious efforts, Christ has come. Give up all that religious work and simply put your trust in Him.

The law made us aware of our sin, and men fainted from the reality of who they actually were. But they were resuscitated by the grace of God, and learned that it is not by "works of righteousness that we have done," but it is by His grace alone.

THE REIGN OF DEATH AND THE REIGN OF GRACE

In Romans 5:14, Paul says, *Nevertheless death reigned from Adam to Moses, even over them that had not sinned after the similitude of Adam's transgression, who is the figure of him that was to come.* Now, please understand that Adam sinned. And that offense has reigned even over those who did not sin like Adam had sinned.

That one offense brought death to all men. They were locked in a prison and could not get out. This is the tragic nature of man's condition, but there is good news in verse 15, *But not as the offence, so also is the free gift. For if through the offence of one many be dead, much more the grace of God, and the gift by grace, which is by one man, Jesus Christ, hath abounded unto many.* Jesus Christ has **abounded unto many**. Just as sin spread over the whole human race, so God's grace is spreading to all who put their trust in Christ. When it comes to a head-to-head confrontation with God's purposes, He will win every time. Sin enters the world, but God counters with His grace, not just a measly portion, but also an abundant portion of grace—enough to cover all of us.

The law says if you're guilty in one part, then you're guilty of the whole thing. In the same way, if you put your faith in Christ, then you are blessed with all things. *And not as it was by one that sinned, so is the gift: for the judgment was by one to condemnation, but the free gift is of many offences unto justification* (Romans 5:16). The law that was based on the one offense is covered by grace. Grace covers many offenses. **The law says if you have one offense you're guilty of the whole law; grace says whether it is one offense or a bunch of offenses you're innocent on all counts.**

It gets better. *For if by one man's offence death **reigned** by one; much more they which receive abundance of grace and of the gift of righteousness shall reign in life by one, Jesus Christ* (Romans 5:17). Everything that Jesus did is enough to give you the ability to walk in the promises of God in this life. "But I'm not perfect," some may say. That's okay. Paul asks, "Was the sacrifice perfect?" The sacrifice was perfect, and because of that, you are free and forgiven. A huge door has been opened for you so that you can rule over all things in your life. No matter what comes into your life, you are more than a conqueror through Christ.

Paul continues in Romans 5:19, saying, *For as by one man's disobedience many were made sinners, so by the obedience of one shall many be made righteous.* It shall be made so. By one man's disobedience many

No matter what comes into your life, you are more than a conqueror through Christ.

were made sinners, but by one man's obedience many shall be made whole. Shall be—that covers you now and tomorrow and next week, if you abide in Him and His words abide in you.

THE LAW SHOWS US OUR NEED OF GRACE

We are coming down the home stretch of Paul's revelation of grace. In Romans 5:20, Paul moves to a critical conclusion. *Moreover the law entered, that the offence might abound. But where sin abounded, grace did much more abound.* He said the law came to make it clear that *we all need grace* because no one can keep the law. We are all under its judgment, and we can't shake ourselves free. The law set a trap and we fell in. We are fenced in by all the commandments. There is no escape… nothing we can do. We are all helpless without grace. In that desperate condition, the grace of God found us and freed us.

That as sin hath reigned unto death, even so might grace reign through righteousness unto eternal life by Jesus Christ our Lord (Romans 5:21). A new law interrupted the reign of sin and

The way of Christ is the way of grace.

death—the law of grace. We are now under a new ruler. The despot of sin has been overthrown, and a new ruler has been put in its place. The new ruler is grace. The way of Christ is the way of grace.

Sin reigned, and now grace reigns until the end of the age. Move over sin, here comes grace. Even in the ages to come, God will continue to unveil the marvel of His grace. Ephesians 2:7 says, *In order that in the ages to come He might show the surpassing riches of His grace in kindness toward us in Christ Jesus* (NASB).

SHOULD WE SIN IN ORDER TO GET MORE GRACE?

What shall we say then? Shall we continue in sin, that grace may abound? (Romans 6:1). Some had been waiting to get to this point. Paul, expecting this kind of reaction, went ahead and tackled this thought straight on. Paul, rather jovially and sarcastically, asked the question, "Shall we continue sinning in order to get more of this marvelous grace?" Paul was attacking two trains of thought.

Paul attacked the abuser of grace who thought that if what he said was true, he could just keep on enjoying sin and getting more grace. Well, Paul said that line of thinking is wrong. It totally missed his point. His response: *God forbid. How shall we, that are dead to sin, live any longer therein?* (Romans 6:2). You don't increase the flow of grace through continual sin. In fact, if you have grace flowing in your life, then it creates a new attitude towards sin. You will not want to sin against the one who has done so much for you.

Paul also wanted to counteract the cynic who was making light of the grace of God by such absurd reactions to his message. Paul has no time for their foolishness and cynical statements. So he put an end to those religious pundits and their ridiculous one-liners. Of course that was not what he was saying.

The man of grace will be able to fulfill the law much better than the one who does not think he needs that grace. The man who is dependent on the law for his salvation will surely fail. But the man of grace will not continue in his sin, for he has been freed from sin.

DEATH TO SIN

If we have died to sin, how can we continue in that sin? That is Paul's argument. Those who have been buried with Christ in baptism have died to sin. They have been released of a sin-consciousness and no longer live in that sin.

> *Know ye not, that so many of us as were baptized into Jesus Christ were baptized into his death? Therefore we are buried with him by baptism into death: that like as Christ was raised up from the dead by the glory of the Father, even so we also should walk in newness of life. For if we have been planted together in the likeness of his death, we shall be also in the likeness of his resurrection.*
> —Romans 6:3-5

If you live under the condemnation of sin, you will always be focused on guilt, shame, inferiority, and condemnation. God says, "I'm going to erase the sin factor and institute the grace factor so that you're free to focus on your wholeness that is a result of Christ's life in you."

Grace is a stream, a cleansing stream of wholeness.

Grace is a stream, a cleansing stream of wholeness. You are free. "But, Pastor..." No, you are free. There's no condemnation to those who are in Christ. So why don't you focus on the grace factor? Why don't you drop on your knees and thank Jesus. He has freed you from bondage to the law so that you can focus on His love and His power that is working in you to make you whole.

Knowing this that our old man is crucified with him, that the body of sin might be destroyed, that henceforth we should not serve sin (Romans 6:6). You are no longer alive to sin. You are no longer controlled by sin. You have died, and your life is now hidden in God. You are forgiven and made whole, so now you can stop the shame game. The focus is no longer the sin that once reigned in your life. The focus is now on how to live your new life in Christ. He has cancelled out all judgment against you as you are now working out your new way of living—living by the grace of God.

Cruising along, Paul continues his discussion in Romans 6:7, *For he that is dead is freed from sin.* Dead men don't sin. Sin is not an option. It is not a focus. God's people do not live their lives trying not to sin. That is not their focus. They are now living lives of joy and peace, with grace pumping through their veins. They are focused on the grace that is coming into their lives. Their eyes are on their Lord who has set them free.

> *Now if we be dead with Christ, we believe that we shall also live with him: knowing that Christ being raised from the dead dieth no more; death hath no more dominion over him. For in that he died, he died unto sin once: but in that he liveth, he liveth unto God.*
>
> —Romans 6:8-10

Sin works in all men, and the result of sin is death! Paul continues his case for the grace factor by saying that if we have been joined to Christ in His death and resurrection, then we have been freed from the power of sin and death. Death's power over you has been eliminated just like the sin problem has been cancelled. Christ conquered the power of death and has taken away its severe sting.

Likewise reckon ye also yourselves to be dead indeed to sin, but alive unto God through Jesus Christ our Lord (Romans 6:11). The word *reckon* means "to take inventory." Let's take inventory of all that we have said. What are the implications of the death, burial, and resurrection of Christ? Take an inventory of your life. Look at all that you have done and just let it die with Christ. Then take an inventory of all that He has done, and let that life now work within you. You are dead because of sin, but you are now alive because of Christ.

Worship is the celebration of these facts. It is a recounting of all that He has done for you. It is the recognition of the greatness of His grace. It is a big "thank you" to God for what we now have because of Jesus.

COORDINATING THE GRACE OF GOD

Let not sin therefore reign in your mortal body, that ye should obey it in the lusts thereof (Romans 6:12). Don't let sin rule and reign in your life. Don't let it be king. Don't obey it; make it obey you. God is not going to wipe you out just because you slipped up and sinned. But He is saying that you should not let sin be a ruler in your house. Don't let it be the king. You belong to another. There is a new king on the throne of your life, and He has imparted to you a grace that is an enabler, empowering you to live righteously and godly before Him.

Neither yield ye your members as instruments of unrighteousness unto sin, but yield yourselves unto God, as those that are alive from the dead, and your members as instruments of righteousness unto God (Romans 6:13). Paul is saying that you need to coordinate the grace of God in your life so that the instruments of your body will serve Him. You must coordinate grace by yielding yourself to God. You once yielded to sin; now you must yield your life to God. Create harmony in your life by allowing grace to be the conductor of your life.

Create harmony in your life by allowing grace to be the conductor of your life.

For sin shall not have dominion over you: for ye are not under the law, but under grace (Romans 6:14). Sin cannot have dominion or exercise lordship over your life as long as you believe in grace, because grace has a cleansing flow. You are no longer controlled by "I can't." You are now controlled by "I will." If you can just trust in the ability that comes by the grace of God, then that trust will release a cleansing stream of grace that will reorder your life.

Know ye not, that to whom ye yield yourselves servants to obey, his servants ye are to whom ye obey; whether of sin unto death, or of obedience unto righteousness? (Romans 6:16). If you keep yielding to sin, it will eventually lead to death. If you keep yielding to obedience, it will eventually turn into full righteousness and wholeness for your life. You're in the middle of something right now. Something is being birthed inside of you. Life is working in you, and you must yield to that new life.

But God be thanked, that ye were servants of sin, but ye have obeyed from the heart that form of doctrine which was delivered you (Romans 6:17). You were once in the crushing clutches of sin, powerless to change your life. Now, since you have been exposed to the doctrine of grace, you have changed. You heard about this grace and responded in faith.

What is the teaching, or doctrine, of grace? It is all about Him and what He has done for us. It instructs us that we now have a new life and new power to live that life. It is a tenderhearted message—a love letter from God to you.

You now recognize that the power you have comes from God. You understand that there is no way to defeat the devil just by telling him to go in Jesus' name. The devil will point at you and say, "You don't have a right to rebuke me." You can only defeat the devil when you stand in grace.

I can hear you saying, "My house is just bound up by sin, and I am not strong enough to change." Yes you are! You are not your own. You have been bought with a price. You now belong to Christ, and He has the power to set you free. There is now enough grace in your life to defeat the devil, death, hell, and the grave.

What fruit had ye then in those things whereof ye are now ashamed? for the end of those things is death (Romans 6:21). The result of sin is shame, and shame is a powerful, negative force in your life. The message of shame is that we feel bad about what we have done. We don't want to live under the rule of sin, but we are powerless over it. The sin we commit creates a certain angst that keeps us depressed about our lives. That is the fruit of sin, and the end of all that is death—the death of a rich life in God.

But now being made free from sin, and become servants to God, ye have your fruit unto holiness, and the end everlasting life (Romans 6:22). When we encountered the grace of God, we found freedom. The power of sin was broken and the sting of shame was eliminated from our lives. We, who were once servants of sin, are now servants of the Most High God. The fruit of sin is shame, leading to death. The fruit of grace is holiness, leading to life.

The fruit of sin is shame, leading to death. The fruit of grace is holiness, leading to life.

Concluding his defense of the message of grace, Paul says in Romans 6:23, *For the wages of sin is death; but the gift of God is eternal life through Jesus Christ our Lord.* The payback on sin is death. You are playing Russian roulette with your life, and the bullet is in the chamber.

The gift of God for those sitting at the table with a gun in their hand is life. Let go of sin and receive the grace of God. It is a gift. It is free. And it is for you. It sounds too good to be true, but it is. Open your life to receive that grace!

Grace
IN ACTION

*For all have sinned and fall short of the glory of
God, and are justified freely by his grace through
the redemption that came by Christ Jesus.*
　　　　　　　　　　　　—Romans 3:23,24 NIV

It really does sound too good to be true, doesn't it? But
the Bible assures us that salvation is a free gift. Our part is to
simply believe it, receive it, and share the message with others.

Having been justified through grace, you must live a life
worthy of His calling. There are many who still need to be
convinced that there is nothing they can do to deserve God's
grace. You can share the good news of the gospel—telling
them that although they can never be good enough to earn
forgiveness, God willingly gives it to all who will believe it
and receive it. Be an ambassador of God's grace in your little
corner of the world.

CHAPTER SIX

THE PARABLE OF A LOVING
FATHER AND HIS PRODIGAL SON

*Let us not love with word or with tongue, but in
deed and truth.*

—1 John 3:18 NASB

*J*ESUS IS THE ULTIMATE EXAMPLE OF LOVE—IN FACT,
THE Bible tells us that He is love. During His ministry
on earth, He often chose to use parables as teaching
tools. Through the parable of the prodigal son, He
conveyed the limitless love of a father for his son.

"The form of the teaching of Jesus, the way in
which he clothes his interior life in words, indu-
bitably possesses an artistic character. The wealth

of the style is remarkable. Jesus could tell a story in a very living, simple and arresting way; he knew how to stir the minds of the hearers with vigour; if necessary he could pour forth scorn with unmistakable energy, he could console with gentleness...be indignant with intense vigour, and rejoice intensely. Everywhere he manifests his creative originality. Everything is brief, every word hits the target, and all is concrete. There is never a word too much. His words always give the impression that they are self-evident. They seem as though they could never be any different from what they are, and this proves that they have issued from within in a living and spontaneous manner."[1]

—Weidel

Jesus was the king of providing biting one-liners at the appropriate moments, and He was, without a doubt, the master storyteller. His one-liners centered on the least, the last, the lost, and the little.

> *"Whoever receives this child in My name receives Me; and whoever receives Me receives Him who sent Me; for he who is <u>least</u> among you, this is the one who is great."*
>
> —Luke 9:48 NASB

> *"But many who are first will be <u>last</u>; and the last, first."*
>
> —Matthew 19:30 NASB

"For the Son of Man has come to seek and to save that which was <u>lost</u>."
—Luke 19:10 NASB

"See that you do not despise one of these <u>little</u> ones, for I say to you, that their angels in heaven continually behold the face of My Father who is in heaven"
—Matthew 18:10 NASB

JESUS—THE MASTER STORYTELLER

"Drawing pictures from their surrounding world, He arrested their minds, stirred their imaginations and moved them to new realms of spiritual reality. Parables were not a new form of communication. For many years they had been an accepted form of communicating spiritual reality. So what made the Jesus stories so different? In his stories, he attacked the conventional wisdom of his day—the accepted psyche of the Jewish community. He reversed religious order, violated accepted social practices, and challenged the motivations of men's actions. In his stories he made the 'bad guys' the 'good guys' and the 'good guys' were made the 'bad guys'. The less honorable were made heroes in the stories of Jesus. The religious leaders were always the villains.

"The only judgment in his stories was against the self-righteous. What was that judgment? They were judged by the Father's love. The compassion of their heavenly Father exposed the hypocrisy of their lives. Be careful what you wish for—the recognition of others, the riches of success, and the rewards of religion. In your attempts to move up the ladder you are actually descending. Pursuit of the first place will put you in the last place."[2]

JESUS, THE PHARISEES, THE RIFFRAFF, AND THREE FANTASTIC STORIES

In Luke 15:1-32, Jesus tells three very powerful stories that center around one of His favorite themes—the lost. He tells about a lost sheep, a lost coin, and a lost son. It was the setting in which Jesus found himself that set His mood for the telling of these dynamic stories. In verse one, we read that the tax collectors and sinners drew near to Jesus. What a mixture—all the riffraff of the society of His day. You wouldn't catch these folks in the modern church of today because they might not expect to feel the love of God there.

There was one other group hanging around. They were always there, standing at the edges of the crowd, waiting to see what Jesus would do when He was in public. Watching this scene, were the Pharisees and scribes, murmuring (that's the language of religious folk) about His actions. What was their problem this time? They were bothered that He was associating with sinners and even eating with them. He welcomed them in His midst, and they couldn't imagine that. Didn't He know that they were *unclean*? To them it didn't matter that He was preaching the gospel to sinners; the important thing was *how* He preached the gospel. They didn't understand that it is the spirit in which you preach the gospel that makes a difference whether people are drawn to God or repelled and pushed away.

It can be the same words but in a different mood. See, the Pharisees made a slanderous statement against Jesus. They said He was a friend of sinners—now, that was meant to be a slam, but Jesus took it as a compliment. Jesus said, "The real question is: Why aren't you a friend of the sinner?" These characters surrounding Jesus, the riffraff and the religious folk, set the mood for Him to start telling stories.

It is important that we understand the reason for these stories. These are not campfire stories without significant meaning. Jesus wanted the religious leaders and the riffraff to understand the love of God and His intense desire to reach out to all men. Jesus explained the significance and the importance of one single individual—the object of His affection.

THE PARABLE OF THE LOST SHEEP

The first parable—a story about a lost sheep—is found in Luke 15:4-6. You know this story. Jesus spoke about a shepherd leaving the ninety-nine sheep and going out to find the one that was lost. Some would say, "Well, a good shepherd would never leave all those sheep just to go out and save one." But Jesus thought differently. He was willing to leave the ninety-nine and go after the one that was lost. Jesus unveiled the heart of God in this story. He told the Pharisees and scribes that it was okay to be part of the ninety-nine. But then He asked, "Why shouldn't I have the freedom to go after that poor lost sheep?"

Indirectly, he said to these Pharisees, "You are already a part of the ninety-nine, so what are you worked up about? You should be out here helping me look for those people who are lost." Jesus concluded the story by saying that the Shepherd went and found the lost sheep, laid the sheep on his shoulders, and brought him home.

There should be some joy and dancing in the house of God when even one who was lost is found.

Jesus got excited about the outcome, and told the religious leaders that there should be some joy and dancing in the house of God when even one who was lost is found.

This is not manufactured joy. This is pure joy flowing from a heart that understands the value of a single person. If you can't get excited about that, then you need to check out your own relationship with God. Jesus went on to say that heaven understands the value of a human soul and so should earth. There ought to be some harmonious joy being produced between heaven and earth at the rescue of those who are lost.

THE PARABLE OF THE LOST COIN

The next parable—the story about a lady who lost a coin—is found in Luke 15:8,9. The whole focus of this parable centers on her frantic search for the coin. We are not talking about a casual search. We are talking about a frenzied and hysterical lady trying to find this coin that evidently meant a great deal to her. She was sweeping and looking everywhere—under the bed and in her dressers—as she desperately tried to find the coin. She was committed to scouring the whole house, and she was not about to give up until she found her precious coin.

The scriptures tell us that she cleaned the whole place. She looked under the furniture and found nothing but hairballs, pennies, and other junk. She swept out every single spot, looking for just that one coin—the lost coin. What's the big deal? The big deal is that the coin had great value and worth to the lady, and she looked everywhere until she finally found it.

Oh happy day! She found her coin. She didn't give up, and neither should we as we seek to find lost souls. Once again, Jesus talks about the joy in heaven over the rescue of the lost. We don't quite have the understanding of the importance of saving a human life. If we did, we would be like the shepherd and the lady. We would not give up until we found what was lost. Every time somebody comes into the house of God and stands under the rain showers of the grace of God, there should be some dancing, rejoicing, and praising. Jesus is saying that there needs to be some joy in the house of God.

THE PARABLE OF THE LOVING FATHER

Now we come to the final parable—the story of a lost son—found in Luke 15:11-32. This story is loaded with paradoxes. It appears that the good son ended up being the bad son, and a bad son turned out to be a good son. Right in the middle of the whole drama is the most important figure in the story—a loving father. The story is traditionally called the Parable of the Prodigal Son. This parable could more appropriately be called the Parable of the Loving Father, because He is the key figure in the story. The story centers on his unique love for both his sons.

One of the interesting things in the story is the vacillation of the two sons. But notice that the father *never changed*. I want you to see this, because most people base their reaction to people on the ups and downs the people go through. Our attitude towards people is affected by how they behave. The most famous of the Jesus stories, this parable illustrates in a most dramatic way the loving heart of Father God, compelling and compassionate.

In this chapter, we see God as a loving father. All of us have a heavenly Father. Whether you had a natural father or not, you have a heavenly Father. I want you to see what a true father's heart looks like, because we all have many different images of a father—images that were developed in our childhood. Even to this day, those images, good or bad, impinge upon

Whether you had a natural father or not, you have a heavenly Father.

our concept of who God is as a Father. This story unveils the true meaning of a father's heart.

At this point, I want to mention two important issues. A lot of people get the word, but they don't get the mood of the word; therefore, it doesn't have the right effect. Or they get the mood of it, but they don't get the right word that goes along with the mood of the word. When you are listening to the voice of God, if you want to increase your accuracy, you must get rid of your own mood. You must dispose of your own nature and attitudes so you can understand God's Word and be able to focus spiritually on what the *mood of God* is in this story. You might get the moral of the story, but I want you to get the mood of the story as well. The mood is the impact of a father's love.

We cannot be prepared for the influx of prodigals until we have experienced the mood of the Father for the lost. When we talk about the love and grace of God, we are talking about the mood of heaven for those who are lost. If we don't have this kind of love, we will never be able to successfully reach a world of lost souls.

We cannot be prepared for the influx of prodigals until we have experienced the mood of the Father for the lost.

THE YOUNGER SON

And he said, "A certain man had two sons: and the younger of them said to his father, Father, give me the portion of goods that falleth to me. And he divided unto them his living. And not many days after the younger son gathered all together, and took his journey into a far country, and there wasted his substance with riotous living. And when he had spent all, there arose a mighty famine in that land; and he began to be in want. And he went and joined himself to a citizen of that country; and he sent him into his fields to feed swine. And he would fain have filled his belly with the husks that the swine did eat: and no man gave unto him. And

when he came to himself, he said, How many hired
servants of my father's have bread enough and to
spare, and I perish with hunger! I will arise and go
to my father, and will say unto him, Father, I have
sinned against heaven, and before thee, and am no
more worthy to be called thy son: make me as one
of thy hired servants.

—Luke15:11-19

The younger of the two sons would not join himself to his father's house because he didn't like the administrations (government) of the house. He decided to go out on his own, and he ended up joining himself to a house that he never wanted to be in. Many of you have found yourself in desperate situations because you made similar decisions. In those tragic places, you also said, "I never thought I would be here." Bad places can always be traced back to bad decisions.

This young man's passion to find approval for his life took him away from the one place where he could find it. His father's love allowed the prodigal the freedom to pursue that approval in other places. The further he got away from his loving father, the closer he got to a "distant country," far from the father's reach. His journey eventually brought him to a lost, lonely, and loveless place.

As we have already discovered, our Father has placed within each one of us an internal mechanism that constantly reminds us of a better place. This homesickness is a fundamental part of the human nature. Our home in the presence of our Father is like a homing beacon that constantly calls us home.

Our home in the presence of our Father is like a homing beacon that constantly calls us home.

"...the ongoing yearning of the human spirit, the yearning for a final return, an unambiguous sense of safety, a lasting home.....But beneath or beyond all that, 'coming home' meant, for me, walking step by step toward the One who awaits me with open arms and wants to hold me in an eternal embrace."[3]

The younger son asked for his inheritance. Now, in that day, there were only two reasons that a young man was given an inheritance. The first was if the father died. The second was if the father was unable to manage his household. When someone comes into the house of God and rejects the Father's love, they are saying one of those two things. But I want you to notice something about the father in this story—he didn't hold a grudge against his son, even though he seemed to be indicating that he didn't believe in his father or what he could provide for him. What would you have done if you had been his father? Most of us would have said, "When you grow up and mature a little more, then we might talk about inheritance." But this father had a different plan.

The father said, "Here, son, I love you anyway, and here's your inheritance." And he didn't even hold a grudge. Well, the boy got the dough and hit the road. He had cash burning a hole in his pocket, and he had a world to see. As long as he had money, he had a lot of friends. And that still happens today— as long as we have something to offer, we will be surrounded by "friends." But what happens when the flow stops? When the money is gone, so are the "friends." The lesson here is that true friendship can never be bought.

Here's the sad part of the young man's story. He never had to leave. While he was in his father's house, he never worried about his money. He never worried about love, acceptance, and forgiveness. He never worried about things like food, clothing, and who would care for him. He knew that whatever blessings the father had belonged to him as well. All his needs were covered as long as he stayed in his father's house. What the son really wanted was freedom to do what he wanted to do. Well, that freedom came at an awful price.

The money ran out, the music stopped, and there was no more food. What's a man to do? Well, the young boy went to work with swine. What a way to make a living. He went from the father's house of blessings to a home in the swine pen. For a Jew, handling swine was the worst thing in the world to be doing.

Many of us are like that. We are sure there must be something out there that will make life easier for us. So here we go down that easy road. But before we know it, we are slopping pigs or working at whatever menial job we can find—simply because we did not understand that with blessing comes responsibility. Nobody wants to hear that "r" word. The father knew that his son had to learn this lesson, and that he would have to learn it the hard way.

Believe me, I know. At an early age, I was called to preach the gospel, but I went away from God. I got on a pro-fighting circuit, and I thought that was the life. But one day I woke up. I came to myself, looked around, and realized that I was living with pigs. I was fighting like a pig, acting like a pig, and everybody around me was talking like pigs. I was fighting conviction every step of the way. My grandmother was calling me all the time, prophesying over me and messing me up! I finally realized that I must return to Father's house.

Perhaps you have taken hold of the reins of your life and gone your own way, and things are not quite working out like you had hoped. Some day, when you look around and see that you have made a mess of your life, you will come to yourself. The first thing you must realize is that you were not meant to live with pigs. Your life is worth so much more. You have a destiny planned by a Father who loves you so very much. He created you, and He has a wonderful plan for your life.

You can come to your senses at the craziest moments. You can be sitting in the middle of a bar half drunk, looking at yourself and your surroundings, and God will come to you and mess you up. Husbands and wives can get into big fights, say things they shouldn't say, and then head for separate rooms. As they're trying to sleep and can't, they begin to wonder why they acted the way they did. After contemplating the situation, they realize that their behavior was way out of line.

When that prodigal son was out there feeding the pigs, he started thinking, and he remembered his father's house and how it used to be. He began to think about the bread at Daddy's house. As he watched the pigs eating corncobs, he began to think of his father's bread.

My grandmother used to send me that bread every day in the form of prayers and intercession. It created a heavenly aroma all around me. Those prayers sustained me until I came to my senses. And the memories of his father's house brought the prodigal son back to a place of sanity.

I believe that on the day he came to his senses, the wind was blowing just right. He caught a whiff of a smell that shook him and made him wake up. It was fresh bread. All of us have been there. We were so far away from home and so spiritually hungry, that we were desperate for our Father's embrace. Longing to hear the sound of His voice, we began to weep because we were so lonely and missed Him so much.

This father was also lonely, wondering what had happened to his wayward boy. He missed him so, and longed to have him back at his side. That's the way it is when we have a desperate need to have God back in our lives. Desperate people do desperate things. They get a little crazy and fanatical in their search for God. They realize that they don't belong with the pigs. They belong in the Father's house.

The Bible tells us that the prodigal son came to himself. He started thinking about the bread at daddy's house. He remembered the wonderful aroma that filled the house when the bread was baking, and he needed some of that bread! Fresh bread brings people back to the house of God. Never underestimate the power of what the Word of God coming out of your spirit can do for another person.

Never underestimate the power of what the Word of God coming out of your spirit can do for another person.

Ah yes, the marvelous power of loving memories. In the midst of his despair, the weary son remembered life in his father's home, and it stirred in him a desire to return. In his efforts to prove himself, the prodigal son had destroyed his life and brought much shame to the family name. Fortunately, his passion to return was more powerful than the shame that covered him.

So the son started preparing his speech for his father. He realized that he had wasted his inheritance, but in a moment of sanity, he realized that even his father's servants had it better than he had it. So the son who had said, "Give me…" was now willing to say, "Make me…". He was ready to go back home and say, "Father, make me like one of your hired servants." This is repentance. He got up, turned his back on the pigs, and put his face towards his father.

THE LOVING FATHER

"And he arose, and came to his father. But when he was yet a great way off, his father saw him, and

*had compassion, and ran, and fell on his neck, and
kissed him. And the son said unto him, Father, I
have sinned against heaven, and in thy sight, and
am no more worthy to be called thy son. But the
father said to his servants, Bring forth the best robe,
and put it on him; and put a ring on his hand, and
shoes on his feet: and bring hither the fatted calf,
and kill it; and let us eat, and be merry: For this
my son was dead, and is alive again; he was lost,
and is found. And they began to be merry."*

—Luke 15:20-24

The closer he got to home, the clearer his memories became.
Father's face was becoming clearer now, and anticipation was
growing. As he crested the hill hiding his home, he saw a
figure running towards him. What he did not know was that
his father had always been waiting. Sitting on the front porch,
he had watched day after day, longing for the return of his lost
son. The father started preparing for the son's return the day
he left home. He wasn't preparing to condemn him. He was
preparing to hold him in his loving
arms. That's the way it is with God.
Every time you go away from God,
He immediately starts preparing for
your return.

*Every time you go away
from God, He immedi-
ately starts preparing
for your return.*

It was a Jewish custom at that
time, that if you were forty years old
or older, you didn't run *for* anything
or *from* anything. You were mature. The checkbook was
balanced. Life was in order, and the family was moving in the
right direction. You weren't supposed to run in public. In that
culture, a servant or someone younger would go out for you,

and if there was urgency for a task to be fulfilled, they would run to fulfill the need.

Seeing his son in the distance, the father lost all his Jewish decorum. Without any concern for what others might think, and with great joy, he ran to meet his beloved son. So it is with God. You think that you are chasing after God, when all along, He has been chasing after you. God comes running after you. God will bypass our rules, regulations, and traditions just to reach out to the least, the last, and the lost. The Father's love overrides a lot of things.

Watching his father running towards him, the son pulled out the paper with his confession and prepared for the coming rendezvous. Heart pounding and lips quivering, he was now ready to humble himself and ask for forgiveness. But an amazing thing happened. As the father reached the son, he grabbed him. Locked in each other's arms, the father began to weep with joy. The son's confession paper was crushed in that loving embrace.

Before the son could speak a word, the father was initiating his own plan. He called to one of his servants, "Get me a robe." He didn't want anyone to see his son in this shocking condition—desperate and destitute.

There are some things that God doesn't want others to see in you, so He will cover you until He can cleanse you. Some things are just between you and God—things that are nobody else's business. Some things don't need to be confessed to a priest or pastor. They are private and personal, and can be handled privately with God. Sometimes things do need to be confessed to others, and healing can come from such confessions. But, on the other hand, there are some things that are only meant for the ears of your Father.

The father of the prodigal son was saying, "I don't want anybody else to know that you looked like this. Put this robe on and everything will be all right. I'm covering you! It's between you and me, and it's nobody else's business." While the son was getting used to this robe of mercy, his father gave him a ring. This wasn't some cheap, insignificant ring. No, this was a signet ring. A family ring—a ring of authority that granted him the privilege of conducting business in his father's name.

In ancient times, when a prodigal returned home, it was customary for the people of the community to follow him home, mocking him and throwing trash at him. But this father would not allow his son to be humiliated and derided by those in the community. With a robe and a ring, they would respect him rather than rebuke him. The robe and the ring had been awaiting the son. The father knew that a day would come when his beloved son would return. He knew that when that day came, he would receive him back with mercy and love and grant him the full privileges of a son. This is the grace factor.

The final act of the loving father was to give his son a pair of shoes for his feet—feet that had been soiled by a life of running from the father. His shoes represented the fact that he had a destiny and a pathway before God that he was predestined to walk in. He had wandered away and lost his direction. But now he was back, and his father would help his son fulfill the original destiny he had planned for him.

When you come back into the house of God after all your wandering, He will receive you, heal you, restore you.

When you come back into the house of God after all your wandering, God will not hold a grudge against you. He will receive you, heal you, restore you, and give you His authority. This is the Father's love.

After the father had welcomed back his son, it was party time. The father told his servant to kill one of his calves and prepare for a glorious barbeque. This was a day for rejoicing, because his son who was lost had returned home. Home had been empty without the son, but now it was full once again. With the smell of barbeque hanging in the air, everyone joined in the celebration. Well, everyone except one person.

THE OLDER BROTHER

"Now his older son was in the field. And as he came and drew near to the house, he heard music and dancing. So he called one of the servants and asked what these things meant. And he said to him, 'Your brother has come, and because he has received him safe and sound, your father has killed the fatted calf.' But he was angry and would not go in. Therefore his father came out, and pleaded with him. So he answered and said to his father, 'Lo, these many years I have been serving you; I never transgressed your commandment at any time; and yet you never gave me a young goat, that I might make merry with my friends. But as soon as this son of yours came, who has devoured your livelihood with harlots, you killed the fatted calf for him.' And he said to him, 'Son, you are always with me, and all that I have is yours. It was right that we should make merry and be glad, for your brother was dead and is alive again, and was lost and is found.'"

—Luke 15:25-32 NKJV

The scene then shifts to an encounter between the father and his eldest son. His son was out working in the field when his younger brother returned home. He was a "good" son, and he was working hard in his father's fields. His day was done, and as he approached home, the sound of music and laughter rang in his ears. *What is going on?* he wondered. He picked up his pace, curious to know the cause for this party noise. Reaching home, he found one of the servants and asked him about the cause for the festivity. On hearing the news, anger filled his heart.

The older brother had no compassion for his younger brother. He resented the fact that he had left home, and he probably resented his father for letting this son get away with such outrageous living. He had watched his father over the years, and he couldn't understand his sadness for his son. As far as he was concerned, his brother was dead.

He would have nothing to do with this scandalous party. The father, realizing that his moody son was not coming in, went out to talk to him. Seeing his father, the son launched into a diatribe against his brother, accusing him of wasting his inheritance in riotous living with harlots.

The Bible doesn't say that the prodigal son spent time with harlots, but that's what the older brother said. As a matter of fact, the older brother never heard the apology of the prodigal. He didn't hear the encounter between his father and brother. He had no idea where his brother had been, and yet he acted like he knew everything.

A critical, judgmental spirit is as bad as a life wasted in lawless living.

When people have a spirit of accusation, they are revealing something about their own hearts. They are unveiling a critical, judgmental spirit that is blocking their own reception of grace and mercy. God never categorizes sin. A critical, judgmental spirit is as bad as a life wasted in lawless living.

This angry brother wouldn't even go in the house. What does that say about him? It says that the reservoirs of his soul were empty and dry. There were no waters of mercy to freshen the life of another. His resentment of his brother opened a river of anger instead of mercy. That's why he didn't go into the house. He was so filled with wrath that he couldn't enjoy the party. In fact, the sounds of the celebration only made him angrier.

But the father was full of grace, and it must extend to the older brother as well. He couldn't allow his older son to remain in that dreadful condition. It was his desire that his older son be able to experience the joy that now filled his heart.

The father went outside looking for the other *lost* son. The older brother immediately commenced with his criticism. "My younger brother wasted his inheritance and dishonored the family. He should pay for his actions. I can't believe that you would simply let him off scot-free."

Watching his father's joy over his brother's homecoming filled him with anger. How could his father just take him back without requiring anything from him? He was the one who had worked hard on Father's behalf. He had not sinned against the family name. He had been a good son, faithfully working for his father.

There are many accounts of jealousy between brothers in the Scriptures. Consider the fatal rivalry between Cain and Abel, the duel that occurred between Ishmael and Isaac, the scandalous actions of Jacob and Esau, and the jealousy that grew in the hearts of the brothers of Joseph. Jealousy has ruined many a good family.

In his account of the older brother of the prodigal, Henri Nouwen said, "There is so much frozen anger among the

people who are so concerned about avoiding 'sin.'"[4] There are too many "older brothers" in the body of Christ who are judgmental and angry over the scandalous nature of the Father's grace and love. His love must change their hearts too. So the Father sent His unique Son into the world to demonstrate His love for all His sons.

THE MORAL OF THE STORY

Remember the crowds—the riffraff and the religious—that surrounded Jesus as He began to tell the three "lost" stories? Jesus was telling the riffraff that they were like the prodigal son. They had gone far away from the Father's house, and now He was calling them home. If only they would come home to the loving arms of the Father, they would receive a robe, a ring, and a shiny new pair of shoes. The Father would cover their shame, give them a ring of authority, and set them on the road with shoes of destiny and purpose.

There was also a message for the religious folks who were listening to the story. To the scribes and Pharisees, Jesus was saying that they were a part of the "backyard boys"—the older brothers. He said, "You are so proud that you work so hard in Father's field. You keep every infinitesimal detail of the law. You are so righteous that you cannot even enjoy a really good party. You are party-poopers. Every time I try to go after a sinner, you get upset about it and cast your disgusting mood over the celebration. Come on now! Lighten up!

"Can't you see that heaven is rejoicing over those who have been found? Don't you see that your judgmental spirit is just as bad as this son's wayward life? Don't you see that all your service—all that religious stuff—is just a cover-up for your lack of grace and mercy? Don't you see that mercy triumphs over judgment? It is my trump card for all that is wrong in your world.

Your works don't earn a relationship with Me. All that I have is already yours. Rejoice for those who had nothing and now have been found. If I want to bless them, what is that to you?"

The Pharisee spirit is never happy. They always want a condition set for those who have wasted their lives. Those who have the smell of pigs on their lives offend them. Not so with the Father. He knows that the smell might not come off in one bath. It might take several baths to get the prodigal good and clean, and it might take some medicine to get rid of the lice in his hair.

This is why the Father established His house among men. God's house is a house of receptivity. You might smell like a sinner, but He covers you with the robe of righteousness anyway and receives you into the place He has prepared for you. Then He dares anyone to open his mouth against anyone that He says is righteous.

Don't judge those who have been washed in His cleansing stream. You might get judged in the process. You better see them the way God sees them!

Don't judge those who have been washed in His cleansing stream. You might get judged in the process.

This is the God you serve. He's always ready and prepared to receive those that others would reject. The world is full of prodigals, and the church of Jesus Christ should be the place where they receive mercy and grace. We must be careful to respond to the prodigals in the right way, because they are God's little ones.

Unfortunately, too many of God's people think that these lost ones need to pay for what they have done. They just don't want them to get off so easy. The Pharisees among us are stunned by the mercy of God that is poured out on such pathetic souls.

Are you ready to receive them back? Or do you want them to have a rough time? Some of you want to send them over to "Pig Pen Christian Center" to get cleaned up first. Let them wallow in the mire for a while, eating husks, and acting silly. But this is not the heart of your Father. Some of us need a heart transplant. The church must again become a home for the wounded, the desperate, the addicts, the prostitutes, and the wayward.

We must extend grace to them. You just never know when you might need a little grace yourself. In the Sermon on the Mount, Jesus announced that the blessed ones are those who are merciful. We live in a time when God is calling prodigals home. Let's prepare a house of mercy for them.

Not only should we be willing to receive them, but like the Good Shepherd, we must be willing to go to the pig pens of the world and help rescue these hopeless souls. They are out there, and they are waiting for somebody to roll that stone away. They need someone to say, "Jesus loves you anyway." You never know what a little grace and mercy might do in the lives of those without God.

You never know what a little grace and mercy might do in the lives of those without God.

God is calling us to forsake the way of the older brother and receive the compassionate heart of the Father. It's a heart of love, compassion, grace, and understanding.

RECEIVE THE LOVE OF YOUR FATHER

Some of you are prodigals. You have wandered off to a distant land, and you just don't know how to get home. You don't know if the Father will receive you. You are afraid of rejection. You keep looking at your life, and you see how you have fallen short.

Your life is consumed by guilt and shame because of your many failures.

I want to assure you today that God has a robe, a ring, and a pair of shoes that were meant for you. Return to Him, and He will receive you into His arms as He covers you with a robe of righteousness. He will wash and cleanse you and then offer you the family ring. It is your ring, designed just for you. It will be your ring of authority that others will soon recognize. Then He will kneel and place those new shoes on your feet—shoes of purpose and destiny. Don't stay where you are any longer. Get up and begin the journey home.

Jesus took all your sins and nailed them to the cross. He has forgiven you, so now you must forgive yourself. He nailed your sins, your problems, and your shortcomings to the cross, and He forgave you and accepted you. He's asking you to do the same right now. This is your day to accept all that the loving Father has prepared for you.

Grace
IN ACTION

…walk worthy of the calling with which you were called, with all lowliness and gentleness, with long-suffering, bearing with one another in love.
—Ephesians 4:1,2 NKJV

The story of the prodigal son is a beautiful story of the love of a father for his wayward son. It is a good lesson for everyone, including you. Too often when people "do us wrong," our human instinct is to be defensive or judgmental. But that's not God's plan. His plan calls for love, gentleness, and longsuffering.

God is still in the business of calling prodigals home. Will you follow the example of the loving father? Will you receive them with love, compassion, grace, and mercy?

CHAPTER SEVEN

GOD IS ON YOUR SIDE

*Not as though I had already attained, either were already perfect: but I follow after, if that I may apprehend that for which also **I am apprehended** of Christ Jesus.*

—Philippians 3:12

You are being apprehended by God! He is in pursuit of you; He is coming after you! Sometimes we have the attitude that God has distanced himself from us, and that He doesn't want to have anything to do with us. We envision a God who is disconnected from our little world. How could He have any concern

for our lives? What we need to understand is that even before the world began, while we were yet sinners, He had a great plan for our lives. He envisioned you in His mind. You see, you have always been on His mind and in His heart. He also saw that you would wander away. Not only you, but all of creation would abandon Him.

Before the first word was spoken from heaven to start the whole creation process, God had a plan, and it included His only and unique Son, Jesus Christ. He said to His Son, "I want You to get up and go after My people." I can imagine Jesus saying, "They don't even know who I am yet." God said, "You get up and go after them anyway, because they will know by the time You get there who I am." At the right time, predetermined by the Father, His Son would enter our world, stripped of any divine advantage, and would apprehend you for His Father's purposes.

What I am trying to tell you is that **God is after you today.** You might not realize it, but He is apprehending you right now. He's involved in your business because He loves you and cares about you. He's after you because He wants to impart victory where there has been defeat, health in place of sickness, a destiny to replace your confusion, and hope for your hopelessness.

Victory in every area of your life—that is His plan for you. He wants you to think and breathe victory. And based on that victory He has given you, He wants you to know the joy of worship that springs forth from a life of triumph. God is not messing around. The Holy Ghost is looking for you. He wants you; He desires you.

He is the hound of Heaven, and even though we may sometimes flee from Him, He follows after us at a peaceful pace until we are apprehended. You cannot escape the reach of the loving arms of the Father. Jesus once said, *"No man can come to me, except the Father which hath sent me draw him: and I will raise him up at the last day"* (John 6:44).

His pursuit is like a magnet pulling you with great force towards His mighty power. He longs to rearrange your life and bring you the peace you long to experience.

His pursuit is like a magnet pulling you with great force towards His mighty power.

You cannot escape Him. Once He has caught your scent, you are done for. He will not relent until you are apprehended. Even in the midst of great personal failure, when we are tempted to flee from Him, there is no place to hide. Just ask King David.

> *"Whither shall I go from thy spirit? or whither shall I flee from thy presence? If I ascend up into heaven, thou art there: if I make my bed in hell, behold, thou art there. If I take the wings of the morning, and dwell in the uttermost parts of the sea; even there shall thy hand lead me, and thy right hand shall hold me. If I say, Surely the darkness shall cover me; even the night shall be light about me."*
> —Psalm 139:7-11

WHAT DOES IT MEAN TO BE "APPREHENDED?"

The word *apprehend* means, "to lay hold, to capture; a mastery; to take, to eagerly possess, to find, to follow after, to overtake, to catch, and to come on to." The Holy Ghost is coming after you today. He is following you, eager to possess you, to capture you and bring you into the fold of the Father's care. He is drawing you into a deeper relationship with Him, saying, "I've got My heart and mind set on you. I've got something for you." You might turn your back and walk away, but He says, "I'm a jealous God, and you're not going to get away that easily, because I am coming after you!"

Some of you know what it means to pursue somebody. Some of you parents have been involved in painful pursuits of your wayward kids, and you will never give up. They are too precious, and you will never retire until they are safely home.

Well, that's what the Holy Ghost is doing; He is pursuing you. Some of you are trying to avoid Him. You are burying yourself in your work or perhaps you are running from Him in your pursuit of all that this world has to offer. You are trying to push Him away, and all He's trying to do is give you victory.

In place of fear, He wants to give you faith. In place of defeat, He wants to give you victory. In place of discouragement, He wants to say, "Here is some courage for you—now get up and be bold in what you're doing." All He wants to do is bring good things into your life.

He's coming after you to give you some of heaven's treasures. He wants to wrap His loving arms around you and give you the spirit of victory today! Jesus Christ wants to take away that spirit of anger and fill you with peace. Some of you think that because of your own personal failures, God will reject you. So you just won't give Him a chance, for fear of rejection. You feel sorry and rotten, but you are too scared to give Him a chance. And still He pursues you.

It doesn't matter how rotten you are, He won't relent and He won't retire. You can ignore Him, avoid Him, snub Him, give Him the cold shoulder, and resist Him, but He continues to pursue you. God is like the Energizer Bunny—He will not run out of energy as He seeks to capture you for His purposes.

He's coming after you with the spirit of righteousness. You can try to hide in the middle of a crowd, but He's watching you. He's got His eye on you, and He will watch you all the way through the crowd. It doesn't matter where you are. You can be across the room, and there He is, looking into your soul. His focus is on you, and He's coming after you.

When you are living in the middle of poverty, He wants to apprehend you with blessings and prosperity. He wants to share with you the riches of heaven. God is saying, "I'm coming after you to give you more than you have now, to make up for all that you lack."

You might be saying, "My mind is all messed up, and I just can't even think right, and I don't really know what's going on." It doesn't matter. He will come after you and give you a sound mind! Allow God to apprehend you. Let Him have complete control of your life! Surrender to Him!

EYES TO SEE AND EARS TO HEAR

He who has an ear, let them hear what the Spirit says to the churches (Revelations 2:11 NASB). Did you know that you have a spiritual ear that can hear the voice of God inside of you? It's called your spirit man. Man is different from all of God's creation in that he was created with a spiritual ear that can hear the voice of God. God loves man and desires to speak to him. But if we could not hear God, how could we know Him? Relationships are based on communication, and communication is based on the ability to speak and hear.

God will speak to you, and He will show you the things that are and the things that are to come. He will explain the present and unveil the future. He will help you make sense of the things that are happening in your life.

In the middle of your turmoil, when you're all caught up in dreadful circumstances, He pursues you in order to rescue you.

He will breathe words of comfort in your ear, saying, "Peace, strength, and courage."

God is not reserved about the grace that He wants to pour out in your life.

He is not holding himself back. God is not reserved about the grace that He wants to pour out in your life. He's coming after you, saying, "I'm going to bless you and you can't hold me back. You can't get rid of Me, because I'm apprehending you for a better life."

Sometimes we try to avoid His still small voice by creating static noise to block it out. We have our televisions blaring and our radios blasting. We are afraid of the sounds of silence. But it is in that inward silence that our souls are drawn into a place where we can experience the renovating power of God's love. Too often our noisy lives are a way of avoiding the deeper questions and concerns that engulf and confuse us. The Holy Spirit apprehends us so that He can remove the clutter of shame and guilt that prevents us from hearing Him whisper sweet things in our ears.

He wants to apprehend you like a policeman would apprehend a suspect. He will chase you down until He can handcuff you with the cuffs of compassion. Yes, God is going to apprehend you. You are a suspect, and once He gets ahold of you, He will bring light into your darkness and change you with His divine life.

He does not see you as others see you. He sees you through eyes of the future. In His eyes, you are already saved, healed, filled, happy, blessed, and set free. Jesus is a divine policeman who is ready to apprehend you for His purposes. He is in hot pursuit, and there is no way you can escape Him.

The Holy Ghost is saying, "You have tried to avoid Me, but guess what? Your brush-off won't work. I'm coming after you, and there is nothing you can do to make Me give up on you. That tactic might work with others, but it won't work with Me." No matter where your flight takes you, He will be there—waiting for you in the most distant places. Go ahead and get mad. Get an attitude. It doesn't matter. You cannot irritate Him or push Him out of the way. He will not give up on you.

God has sent His Holy Spirit after His children, saying, "Pursue them and make sure they are blessed, happy, free, and walking in My Spirit in every area of their lives." God is more committed to arresting you than you are to abandoning Him.

God is more committed to arresting you than you are to abandoning Him.

So if you have ears to hear the Spirit of the Lord today, He will speak to you. You just need to turn down the noise and tune your ear towards heaven. Shut your eyes for a moment, focus on your needs, and let the word of the Lord calm your soul. If you have turmoil, you need to hear a word of peace. If you are confused, you need to hear a word of wisdom. If you are in pain, you need to hear a word of healing. You need to hear what the Lord has to say. There is nothing wrong with getting advice from others and hearing their perspective, but it is never, ever a substitute for **you** hearing God for yourself. No one can hear God for you. Tune out all the other voices and open your spirit man to hear God's voice.

What will God say if you are able to hear Him? God will speak victory into your spirit. God will speak soundness into your mind. God will speak joy in the middle of your depression! He will speak strength in the midst of your weakness. He will speak healing into your hurting places. When you are feeling hatred or irritation, God will begin to speak love into your circumstances. God will speak what you need to hear.

GOD IS ON YOUR SIDE!

Then the king of Syria warred against Israel, and took counsel with his servants, saying, In such and such a place shall be my camp. And the man of God sent unto the king of Israel, saying, Beware that thou pass not such a place; for thither the Syrians are come down. And the king of Israel sent to the place which the man of God told him and warned him of, and saved himself there, not once nor twice. Therefore the heart of the king of Syria was sore troubled for this thing; and he called his servants, and said unto them, Will ye not shew me which of us is for the king of Israel? And one of his servants said, None, my lord, O king: but Elisha, the prophet that is in Israel, telleth the king of Israel the words that thou speakest in thy bedchamber. And he said, Go and spy where he is, that I may send and fetch him. And it was told him, saying, Behold, he is in Dothan. Therefore sent he thither horses, and chariots, and a great host: and they came by night, and compassed the city about. And when the servant of the man of God was risen early, and gone forth, behold, an host compassed the city both with horses and chariots. And his servant said unto him, Alas, my master! how shall we do? And he answered, Fear not: for they that be with us are more than they that be with them. And Elisha prayed, and said, LORD, I pray thee, open his eyes, that he may see. And the

LORD opened the eyes of the young man; and he
saw: and, behold, the mountain was full of horses
and chariots of fire round about Elisha.

—2 Kings 6:8-17

The Syrians were at war with Israel. Every time the king of
Syria plotted a new strategy against Israel, Elisha would tell the
king of Israel where they were. This didn't happen just once or
twice but several times. The Syrian king was getting quite frus-
trated. He was sure that there must be a spy who was helping
Israel, so he asked his servant to find him. The servant soon
returned to inform the king that there was no mole, but a
prophet.

Well, the king understood that if he was ever going to defeat
Israel, he must first take care of the prophet. So He found out
that the prophet of God was in Dothan, and sent his army to
Dothan to capture the prophet Elisha. During the night, the
armies of Syria surrounded the city. Early the next morning,
Elisha's servant, Gehazi, woke up and took his early morning
walk. Reaching the edge of the city, he saw a whole host of
Syrians. The servant's heart sank, and he ran to find his master.
"What will we do?" he asked. Without any fear of the situation,
Elisha told Gehazi, "No problem." You see, Elisha saw something that Gehazi didn't see. Seeing the fear in Gehazi's eyes
and feeling sorry for him, he asked the Lord to open the young
man's eyes. Gehazi's eyes were opened, and what a spectacular
sight he saw. On the mountains was another army—the army
of the Lord. Everything was going to be okay.

The first important thing in this story is that there was a
prophet in Israel who had his ears attuned towards heaven.
There was no static noise in his spirit. The dial of his inner ear

was tuned in to heaven's station. God spoke to him and warned him about the movements of the Syrians.

What God did for Elisha, He will do for you. The enemy is trying to destroy your life. He is committed to bringing you down. But the Spirit of the Lord is trying to reveal to you the plots that the enemy is conspiring against you.

A lot of times, we just look at the surface of what is going on in our lives. We look at the circumstances, not understanding that our battle is not with flesh and blood, but against principalities, powers, rulers of darkness, and spiritual hosts of wickedness (see Ephesians 6:12).

If you will just listen, God will tell you how you should pray and what demonic spirits you need to war against. God is right there with you. He has not left you alone and vulnerable. He loves you, and His grace is ready to empower you against all the ploys of the enemy. He has given you the spiritual weapons of war that you need to pull down everything that is warring against you. Whatever it is, you need to stand up to that thing in the authority of Jesus Christ and say, "I bind your power!" Christ has given you that authority and that power. He is on your side.

God will show you how the enemy is working. He will show you the devil's plan for sneaking into your life and attacking you. He will show you how to recognize the devil's patterns. The enemy depends on deceit, but God will counter His deceit with the Truth.

Sometimes you will find yourself in the middle of a very bad situation, with no idea of how you got there or how to get out. But in the midst of trying to figure out what you should do, you can hear that still small voice giving you direction. You have heard that voice before, and you are familiar with its owner. He speaks. You listen. Then it all becomes clear, and you know exactly what to do. What a wonderful God we serve! He is on our side, and if He is for us, then we will be victorious.

The Bible says that one of the jobs of the Holy Spirit is to show us things to come. *"Howbeit when he, the Spirit of truth, is come, he will guide you into all truth: for he shall not speak of himself; but whatsoever he shall hear, that shall he speak: and he will shew you things to come"* (John 16:13). When you open your spiritual eyes, God will show you what you need to see. You can reach out and by the power of the

When you open your spiritual eyes, God will show you what you need to see.

Holy Spirit, put a stop to the devil's dastardly deeds.

You don't have to stay in a cycle of failure! You can break out of it right now. God wants to show you how to stop the sequence of suffering that has surrounded your life. He is for you. All you have to do is stop and listen. God wants to speak to you and reveal His secrets for your success. You may feel like you are alone, but you are not.

YOU ARE NOT ALONE

All of us have felt the sinking feeling that we are alone. We were created for community, and when we find ourselves isolated from others, it is a horrible feeling. But we have strength and peace when we know that others are standing with us. The darkness created by personal pain, whether physical or emotional, makes us want to cry out, "My God, why have You forsaken me."

This is another devious tactic of the enemy. He will do his best to convince you that you are alone, but you are not alone. Whether you feel God or not, He is with you, longing to embrace you and speak to you. The problem is that you are allowing the clatter created by your sorrow to drown out His voice. The best thing you can do is to find a quiet place, shut down the noise, and open your inner ear to the voice of God.

Hearing His voice will counteract all the false information that is coming to you from the exterior world—information that says you are a failure, that you are no good, and that you will never outlast this time of your life. Gradually God's words begin to drift in, and you begin to understand that with Him on your side, you will make it. Suddenly you realize that you are not alone, and you know that with His help, you will survive this moment.

If we will listen to the Spirit of the Lord on the inside, we will understand what is really going on. Sometimes, when we get a *word* from God, we envision how that *word* will play out in our lives. And when it doesn't happen exactly as we had hoped, we allow despair to take over. We must understand the importance of trusting God to bring forth His own *word,* in His own *time,* and in His own *way.* You must learn to listen with discernment and then respond in trust. We must not allow our circumstances to control our lives. Sometimes we have to walk through troubling places to get to the place promised by the Father. So no matter what you go through, remember that the Father will bring you home.

CIRCUMSTANCES!

Success in life is determined by how we deal with the unpredictable circumstances that creep into our lives. Being able to hear the Lord's voice in the middle of troubling situations is not always easy. Sometimes we think that if we could just get away for a while, all our troubles would go away. If we could escape to another place and get out of the fire, then everything just might go away. Our human nature always wants to take a vacation or escape from our trials.

This urge to escape is natural. None of us like being in the fire. But escape is not the answer. Learning to hear God in the midst of the fire is a lesson that all of us must learn. We cannot always run away. Rarely can we take a break from life to try to figure out what is going on. So in the midst of our misery, we must seek an answer from God. We just can't put life on pause and hope everything will work out. No one has that luxury.

Put yourself in the circumstances that Gehazi was facing. You have a fierce army staring you in the face, and you can't run and hide. Gehazi could only see the circumstance, and it didn't look good. What does one do? Well, you need a new set of eyes—eyes that can see the invisible. Elisha had those eyes, and when he prayed that the Lord would open the eyes of Gehazi, it happened. Gehazi got a new set of eyes that enabled him to see what Elisha saw. He saw that there was another mighty army on guard to protect God's children.

No matter what your circumstance, God is trying to apprehend you. He is using your circumstances to capture you so that He can change you. When you are caught up in worrying about your situation, you overlook the fact that you are not alone. A great army is surrounding you. The Lord of hosts is with you, and He has positioned a garrison of angelic hosts to help you out!

The Lord of hosts is with you, and He has positioned a garrison of angelic hosts to help you out!

If God be for you, who can be against you? You need to know that you are more than a conqueror in Christ Jesus. It may seem as though you have heard that a million times, but it is true. And that truth needs to be massaged into your being.

You are the head, and not the tail. You are blessed in your coming in and going out! That is what the Spirit of the Lord is speaking to you. Just open your ears and you will be surprised what you will hear.

PRAYER

> *Lord Jesus, give me a new set of eyes so that I can see what You have prepared for me. Apprehend me, God. I surrender! Come into my life in a greater way. Show me the strategies that the devil is plotting against me. I thank you, Lord, that I am more that a conqueror through You today.*
>
> > *In Jesus' name I pray. Amen.*

Grace
IN ACTION

If God is for us, who can be against us? He who did not spare His own Son, but delivered Him up for us all, how shall He not with Him also freely give us all things?

—Romans 8:31,32 NKJV

The enemy is alive and well, and he's making his last-ditch effort to convince people that they are on their own, that God doesn't really care about helping them. But nothing could be further from the truth. Jesus came to apprehend us and impart victory where there has been defeat.

Remind yourself and others that the enemy operates in deceit, but God overcomes deceitfulness with truth. Never forget that in the fight against the devil, God is on your side. And with God on your side, you will always be victorious.

CONCLUSION

GRACE IN THE POSTMODERN WORLD

Of His fullness we have all received, and grace upon grace.

—John 1:16 NASB

W E LIVE IN AN EVER-CHANGING WORLD. CHANGE, happening at hyper-drive speeds, is the nature of the postmodern world. This change is impinging on every area of our lives. Many have been proclaiming for years that we have entered into the postmodern age. The modern world was influenced secularly by the enlightenment and religiously by the reformation. Many see the '60s as a real turning point in our culture. During that time, the old culture was challenged. Drugs, free love, protest, cynicism, and distrust for authority created new colors for the culture.

Now that we have turned the corner into the twenty-first century, a new cultural philosophy has begun to take root. The new culture emphasizes the individual, uncertainty of absolutes, tolerance, primacy of reasoning, the rejection of the supernatural, and an entrenched distrust of all authority. People are disenchanted with the political world that is plagued by scandal, lies, self-promotion, and insensitivity. Many have been disillusioned by the church that is embroiled in theological conflict, sometimes viewed as intolerant and irrelevant, and often speckled by its own scandals in leadership. Most are fearful of the world they live in—a world that is dominated by the threat of terrorism, facing the possibility of inevitable natural disasters, and watching the rise of all kinds of modern diseases.

The modern man struggles to resolve the conflict between deep personal desires for spiritual reality with an equally extreme uncertainty over whether such a reality exists.

If we as believers and the church really care about humanity, then we must pause to ponder the meaning of this postmodern phenomenon. We cannot simply ignore this shift in our culture and pretend that it does not exist. If the church is going to avoid the indictment of irrelevancy and turn the tide, she must begin to be engaged in an honest evaluation of her effectiveness in exposing men and women to the radical nature of God's love for them.

The answer to the human predicament is found in the grace factor. As I have said throughout this book, when you factor grace into the human equation, there is hope for the human predicament. Grace enters the darkness of our world and brings a new light of hope shining into the crevices of our dismal life.

It is only when you understand the tragedy of the human dilemma that you can truly understand the value of God's grace. Grace enters into our world and rearranges our thinking and acting. This is the grace factor.

Grace looks at the human equation and calls things that "are not" as though "they are." The eyes of grace see you and judge you in a different way and by a different criterion than men do. Man looks on the outward appearance, but God looks on the heart. This is the grace factor, and it is the new power that will attract the postmodern man.

It's not dependent on what we can do or can't do, but it is dependent on what God can do through us. This is the grace factor. God wants to get His grace *to* you so that He can get His grace *through* you to others. Grace is a river, not a lake, and God's desire is that your life will be a river that will allow grace to flow into the lives of those who are cynical, in bondage, lonely, and desperate.

We live in a dark world that is dominated by fear and failure, but the grace factor overcomes the fear factor and resolves the sin factor. The grace factor is based on the nature of God and His love for you. He is the initiator and you are the recipient. The grace factor is Jesus. When you are looking for grace, you will find it at the feet of Jesus.

The grace factor overcomes the fear factor and resolves the sin factor.

Many people in this world have never felt the tenderness of His affection, the magnitude of His grace, and the hush of His mercy. The church is called to be a conduit of that grace to the postmodern man who does not believe in the truth of the supernatural. We must help man disentangle his dilemma of doubt and fear. We will need to give man's image of God an extreme makeover according to the true biblical image. There is nothing wrong with who God is, but there are serious problems with who men think God is.

Modern man is plagued with a distorted image of God. They see Him as an angry, vengeful God. Why would men and women want to approach such a God? How could they love Him? We must first change the image that exists in many of us so that we can correct that image in others. We must allow people to see the goodness and the grace of God, not only through our words but, most importantly, through our actions.

We don't need a glitzy marketing campaign with witty words in order to attract the world to buy our product. All we have to do is manifest to them the God who is here, the God who loves them. We must overcome our own faulty images of God so that the reality of who He is will be delivered to others in a fresh, new way that has the scent of authentic truth. Before we can overwhelm others with the truth of who God is, we must first be overwhelmed anew ourselves by the mighty, outrageous love of God.

If the love of God is to be real in a skeptical world that has lost faith in the church, then it must be through a dynamic love that will reach out in gentle care for those who have gone through the tragedy of divorce, the pain of disappointment, the abuse of drugs, the bondage of poverty, the horror of physical and sexual abuse, and the sting of rejection. Rather than to bring judgment on them, we have been called to love them, support them, heal them, and lead them to the green pastures where they will discover the compassionate Great Shepherd.

This is the grace factor—the one factor that can put a new face on the believer and the church and cause us to be the city of refuge that God designed us to be—a refuge for the broken, the destitute, the poor, the disenfranchised, and all who are searching for spiritual truth.

NOTES

Chapter 1: The Grace Factor

1. Buechner, Frederich, *Telling the Truth*, (Harper Publishers, San Francisco, 1977) 42.

2. Manning, Brennan, *The Ragamuffin Gospel*, Multnoma, Sisters, Oregon, 1990) 25.

3. Capon, Robert Farrar, *The Romance of the Word*, (Eerdmans Publishing, Grand Rapids, Michigan, 1995) 8.

Chapter 2: What Is So Amazing about Grace?

1. Capon, Robert Farrar, *The Fingerprints of God*, (Eerdmans Publishing, Grand Rapids, Michigan, 2000) 11,12,15.

2. Milam, Don, *The Ancient Language of Eden*, (Destiny Image Publishers, Shippensburg, PA, 2003) 121,122.

3. Ibid, 127.

4. Tillich, Paul, *The Shaking of the Foundations*, (Charles Scribner's Sons, New York, 1948) 161.

Chapter 3: The Workings of Grace

1. Goguel, Maurice, *The Life of Jesus,* (Macmillian, New York, 1954) 561,562.
2. Tillich, Paul, *The Shaking of the Foundations,* (Charles Scribner's Sons, New York, 1948) 156.

Chapter 4: The Power of Grace

1. Milam, Don, *The Ancient Language of Eden,* (Destiny Image Publishers, Shippensburg, PA, 2003) 73.
2. Asimakoupoulos, Greg, "For the Hunger in Your Heart," *Decision Magazine,* March 1994, V. 35, No. 3.
3. Capon, Robert Farrar, *The Fingerprints of God,* (Eerdmans Publishing, Grand Rapids, Michigan, 2000) 38.
4. Murren, Doug, "Growth and Mistakes," *Ministries Today,* Mar./Apr. 1994, V. 12, No. 2.
5. Jernigan, Jeff, "Leadership, What's It All About?" *Discipleship Journal,* Jul./Aug. 1993.

Chapter 5: Grace—Just Seems Too Good to Be True

1. http://www.trekker.co.il/english/mount-of-olives.htm.
2. Tillich, Paul, *The Shaking of the Foundations,* (Charles Scribner's Sons, New York, 1948) 161,162.

Chapter 6: The Parable of a Loving Father and His Prodigal Son

1. Goguel, Maurice, *The Life of Jesus* (The MacMillian Company, New York, 1953) 281.
2. Milam, Don, *The Ancient Language of Eden* (Destiny Image Publishers, Shippensburg, PA 2003) 103, 104.
3. Nouwen, Henri, *The Return of the Prodigal Son,* (Doubleday, New York, 1992) 6.
4. Nouwen, Henri, *The Return of the Prodigal Son,* (Doubleday, New York, 1992) 71.

ABOUT THE AUTHOR

Dr. Barry Cook is the senior pastor of Ambassador Family Church in Oceanside, California, a diverse, multi-racial church with over 22 nations represented. Dr. Cook has an earned doctorate degree in Christian Leadership and Church Growth, and is the president and founder of Ambassador Leadership Institute, an accredited Bible college that offers both undergraduate and graduate degrees.

An international speaker, Dr. Cook provides leadership and teambuilding skills to companies and churches worldwide in two-day seminars through his corporation, The Leader's Edge. His approach is fresh, interactive, and reaches across racial and cultural boundaries.

THE LEADER'S EDGE

The Leader's Edge is a newsletter on leadership, written and distributed by Dr. Barry Cook. Leadership is the most precious commodity in today's world, and those who posses it have an uncommon EDGE for success, promotion, and influence. Sign up for *The Leader's Edge* newsletter at:

www.ambassadorfamily.com/leadership

Ambassador Ministerial Association—Raising up ministers with a spirit of revival and reform. For more information go to:

www.ambassadorAMA.net

Contact Information

For more information on Ambassador Family Church, or to contact Dr. Barry Cook, please visit our Web site at:

AmbassadorFamily.com

Or by mail:
Ambassador Family Church
1602 El Camino Real
Oceanside, CA 92056